MW00939046

THE POWER
OF CHOICE

The Greater Adventures of

HUMPTY DUMPTY

Written by

Joyce Guccione

The Power of Choice
Copyright 2007
by Joyce E. Guccione

The Greater Adventures of Humpty Dumpty
Copyright 1995
by Joyce E. Guccione

Illustrations by Steve Hrehovcik

Optimystic Minds, Inc.
4238B N. Arlington Heights Road
Arlington Hts. IL 60004.

Published by Lulu 2007

ISBN 978-1-4303-1741-8

Printed in the United States of America.

THE POWER OF CHOICE

To Susana—
May each day be
better than the last!

Acknowledgment

Inspiration is all around us. We need only to recognize and accept it. I wish to acknowledge the tremendous contributions others have made to my life by always encouraging me in all that I have done. I also wish to thank those who have *discouraged* me for *they* have motivated me to succeed in spite of them!

Contents

The GREATER Adventures
Of Humpty Dumpty
1

Words of Encouragement
33

Picking up the Best
235

Leaving All the Rest
254

Annotated Index
258

Epilogue
290

This book is dedicated to all those who have ever

fallen from their wall,

stumbled on their path,

or have gotten muddied up.

The Greater Adventures of HUMPTY DUMPTY

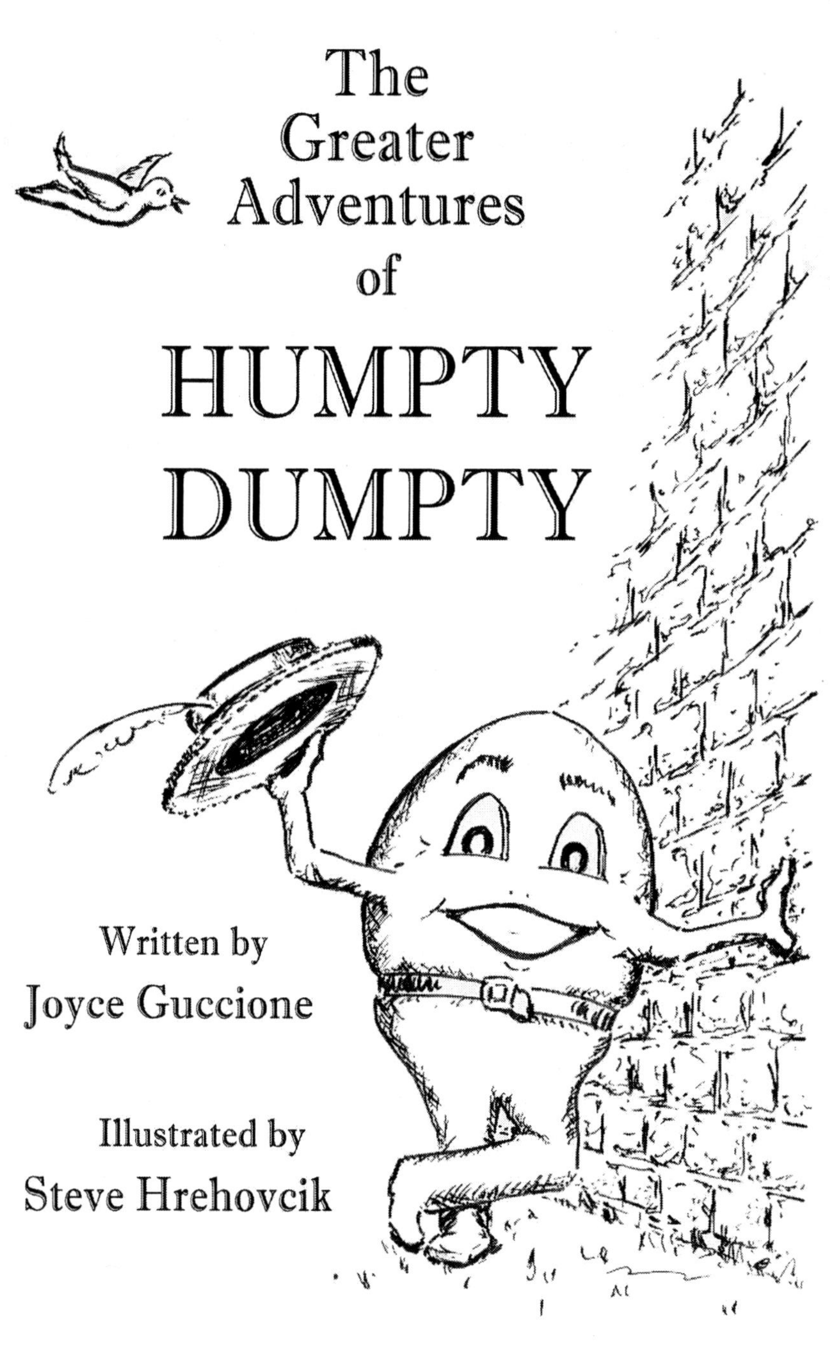

Written by
Joyce Guccione

Illustrated by
Steve Hrehovcik

The Untold Story of The Greater Adventures of ***Humpty Dumpty***

I am quite sure that you are familiar with the story of Humpty Dumpty. The original version was a tragic story which left the protagonist alone and defeated in the end. As a sensitive child, it troubled me deeply to think of the hopelessness of H.D.'s situation. I was bothered by "all the King's horses and all the King's men" giving up and leaving poor Humpty there scrambled!

I often mused about "the rest of the story" and, being the optimist that I am, I was sure that there was a "happily ever after" in it somewhere. At long last, like a misplaced chapter, here are the "Greater" Adventures of Humpty Dumpty and yes, Virginia, there ***is*** a happily ever after!

Humpty Dumpty sat on a wall...

Humpty
Dumpty
had
a
great
fall!

All the King's horses
and all the King's men
couldn't put Humpty
together again.

Humpty Dumpty
sat in the mud.

Humpty Dumpty
felt like a dud!

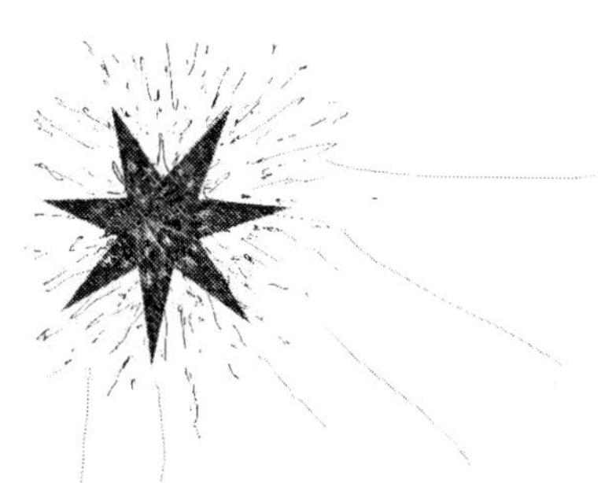

All of a sudden
he heard a small voice,

Whispering loudly
that he had a choice.

"You can sit in the mud...
You can feel like a dud."

"A dud in the mud,
all covered with **crud.**

"You do not have
to sit in the mud."

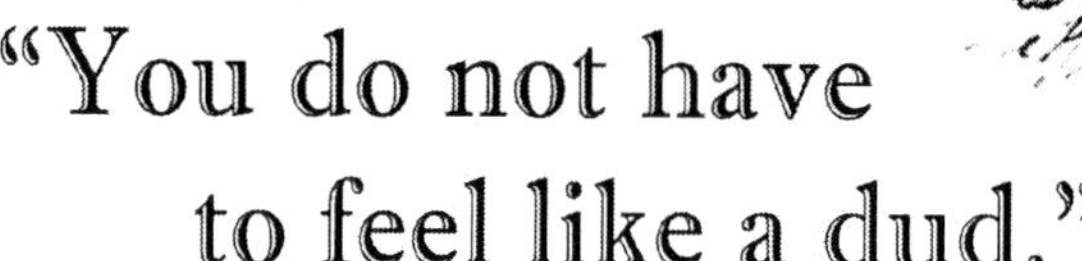

"You do not have
to feel like a dud."

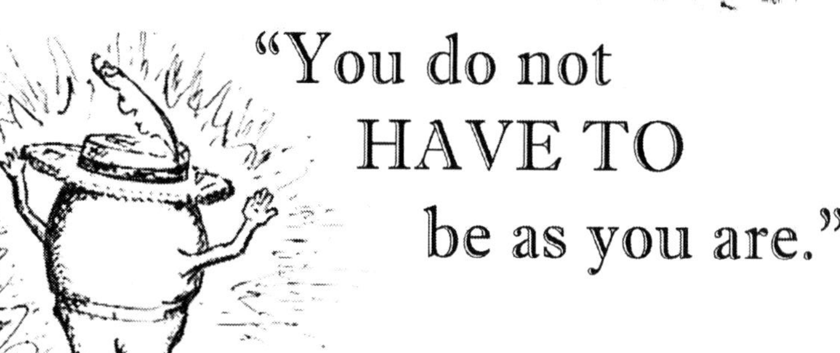

"You do not
HAVE TO
be as you are."

"Listen
to me...

"You can go far."

Humpty Dumpty
listened in pain.

Humpty Dumpty
wanted to gain.

All of his pieces
and all of his heart
wanted to put it
together and start.

"You can pick up the best,"
said the Voice.

"You can leave all the rest.
It's your choice."

FAR

"You do not have to
be as you are."

"Listen to me and
you will go far."

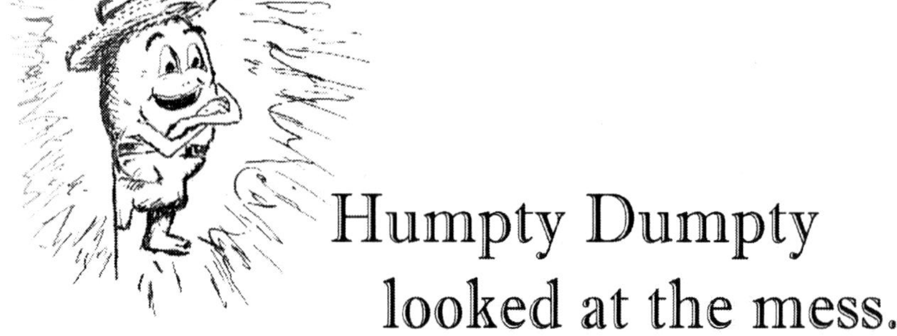

Humpty Dumpty
looked at the mess.

Humpty Dumpty
saw he was blessed.

All of his worries
and all of his woes

He'd leave on the floor
like an old set of clothes.

"You can rise
up so 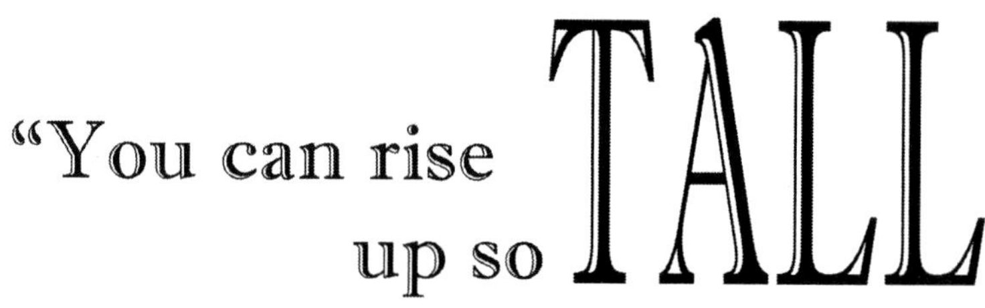

You can
stand like a WALL

As tall as a wall
Most better than all!"

"You can think with
your brain........

"You can dance
in the rain."

"A brain in the rain,
All ready to gain."

"You **DO NOT** have
to be as you are.

Listen to me and
you can go FAR

"You can stand like a wall."
said the voice.

You can dance in the rain.
It's your choice."

"You can think
what you are.
You can think
you'll go far.

You can reach for a star,
then a STAR you are!"

"Never again you'll
sit in the mud...

Never again you'll
feel like a dud."

MUD
DUD

"You do not have to
be as you are.

Listen to me and
you will go far."

Humpty Dumpty
heard what it said.
Humpty Dumpty
got a new head.

All the King's horses
and all the King's men
Couldn't believe it was
Humpty again!

HD

Humpty Dumpty
felt like a king.
Humpty Dumpty
had a new thing.

All of the sudden
he said to the voice
"What is your name?"

It said,
"I am your CHOICE."

Words of Encouragement

We are called to heal the broken,
to be hope for the poor.

Where seldom is heard
a discouraging word,
the skies are not cloudy all day.

Encouraging Words

In times of despair, illness or tragedy, it is the compassionate and caring thing to send the afflicted one a greeting card or a note with our words of encouragement. The following is a collection of true and actual quotations. While these quotations may not have been specifically intended for Humpty Dumpty, they do seem appropriate as messages of consolation and encouragement intended for "H.D." as he struggled to unscramble himself.

Perhaps these original quotations were spoken or maybe they appeared as a card on a floral arrangement. They may have been written as a well appointed letter or as a note scribbled upon a napkin. They may even have been part of a great speech. In the preparation of this manuscript, the quotations have curiously arrived at my desk and almost seemed to arrange themselves for inclusion in this book. They are herein presented as H.D.'s scrapbook of quotations. They record well wishes, not only for H.D., but most importantly for you, the reader! A brief but detailed biographical index of those quoted will follow to give further insight into their own trials and tribulations as well as their own personal issues.

A curious phenomenon seems to occur to who those take the time to read the quotations. A few minutes spent in reading the litany of quotes is said to have an uplifting effect upon the reader. The quotations truly seem to be "Encouraging Words" which work well to empower the Humpty Dumpty in each of us. For those who have fallen off of a wall, for those who are sitting in the mud or who are feeling like a dud, for those who have gotten "covered with crud", may I present some Encouraging Words:

"You have vast undamaged areas within yourself!
No matter what life has done,
no matter what you have done;
the renewal power is there within you.
If you bring spiritual power
to bear upon those undamaged areas,
you can rebuild life,
no matter what has happened to it."

Dr. Norman Vincent Peale

*"Although we don't always have a choice
in what happens to us,
we really DO have a choice
in how we react to what's happened."*

Jane Seymour

"Our greatest glory is not
in never falling,
but in rising every time we fall."

Confucius

"Do or do not.
There is no try."
Yoda

"Failure is unimportant.

It takes courage to make a fool of yourself."

Charlie Chaplin

"To enjoy good health,
to bring true happiness to one's family,
to bring peace to all,
we must first discipline and control one's own mind.

If a man can control his mind,
he can find the way to Enlightenment,
and all wisdom and virtue
will naturally come to him. "

BUDDHA

"There is nothing in a caterpillar
that tells you it is going to be a butterfly."

"Most of my advances were by mistake.
You uncover **what IS**
when you get rid of **what ISN'T**."

R. Buckminster Fuller

"Whatever problems you have,
there's somebody out there who
has overcome something similar
in his or her life.
And if they can,
you can too!"

"Make peace with your past
and get over it."

Oprah

"When life knocks you down,
you should always try to land on your back,
because if you can LOOK UP,
you can GET UP!"

Les Brown

"Every moment of your life is infinitely creative
and the universe is endlessly bountiful.
Just put forth a clear enough request,
and everything your heart desires
must come to you."

Shakti Gawain

"Don't cling to the past:
Not through regret,
Not through longing.
To do so is to tie yourself to a memory,
for yesterday is gone.

It is wisdom to profit
from yesterday's mistakes…
Yesterday's experiences are the Foundation
on which you build today."

Conrad Hilton

*"BE WISER THAN OTHER PEOPLE IF YOU CAN,
BUT DO NOT TELL THEM SO."*

Lord Chesterfield

"Be of good cheer.
Do not think of to-day's failures,
but of the success that may come to-morrow.

You have set (yourself) a difficult task,
but you will succeed, if you persevere:
And you will find joy in overcoming obstacles-
A delight in climbing rugged paths
Which you would perhaps never know
if you did not slip backward...

Sometime, somewhere, somehow
we shall find that which we seek."

Helen Keller

"Don't compromise yourself.

You are all you've got...

Sometimes people are shocked when I say

I am *glad* that my crisis enveloped me,

but I have the feeling

I'd never have known I could be so happy

if I hadn't gone through the bad part...

I think you have to experience some lows

in order to appreciate your highs.

Everybody suffers doubts,

everybody has emotional setbacks,

but right now... try to live a day at a time.

And when that isn't possible,

an hour at a time.

And sometimes, just a minute at a time."

Betty Ford

"You have to accept whatever comes
and the only important thing is that
you meet it with courage
and with the best you have to give.

Remember,
no one can make you feel inferior
without your consent."

Eleanor Roosevelt

"Believe deep down in your heart
that you're destined to do great things."

Joe Paterno

"Aerodynamically the bumble bee shouldn't be able to fly, But the bumble bee doesn't know it so it goes on flying anyway."

Mary Kay Ash

"Most people are about as happy as they make up their minds to be."

Abraham Lincoln

"Nothing in life is to be feared.

It is only to be understood."

Madam Curie

`Where there is LOVE there is LIFE. . .`
Mohandas Gandhi

"Opportunities are disguised by hard work,

so most people don't recognize them."

Ann Landers

"The more sand has escaped

from the hourglass of our life,

the clearer we should see through it."

Niccolo Machiavelli

"If you always put a limit
on everything you do,
physical or anything else,
it will spread into your work
and into your life.

There are no limits.
There are only plateaus
and you must not stay there.

You must go **BEYOND** them."

Bruce Lee

"Failure seldom stops you.

What stops you is FEAR of failure."

Jack Lemmon

"I've had GREAT success being a total idiot."

Jerry Lewis

"LET US NOT LOOK BACK IN ANGER
NOR FORWARD IN FEAR,
BUT AROUND IN AWARENESS."

James Thurber

"EVEN NAPOLEON HAD HIS WATERGATE."
"IT AIN`T OVER TILL IT`S OVER."

Yogi Berra

"If you look closely enough,
amid the merciless and the bitter,
there is always the chance
that you may find comfort and
the promise of something good."

Bob Greene

"I've had many troubles
but the worst of them never came."

James A. Garfield

*"The time for action is NOW.
It's never too late to do something."*

Antoine de Saint-Exupery

"A man is a success
if he gets up in the morning
and goes to bed at night
and in between
he does what he wants to do."

Bob Dylan

"Living is a constant process
of deciding
what we are going to do."

Jose Ortega y Gasset

"MISTAKES are portals of DISCOVERY."

James Joyce

"Those who stand for nothing,

fall for anything."

Alexander Hamilton

"Accept everything about yourself-

I mean everything you are and

that is the beginning and the end-

No apologies, No regrets."

Henry A. Kissinger

"If you don't believe in yourself

then who will believe in you?"

Michael Korda

"It's unbelievable how much you don't know

about the game you've been playing all your life."

Mickey Mantle

"Stumbling is not falling."

Malcolm X

"Don't be afraid your life will end,

be afraid that it will never begin."

Grace Hansen

"The reward for work well done

is the opportunity to do more."

Jonus Salk

"Being a princess isn't all it's cracked up to be."

Princess Diana

"DON'T give up.

DON'T lose hope.

DON'T sell out."

Christopher Reeve

"Failures are fingerposts on the road to achievement."

C. S. Lewis

"The best luck of all
is the luck
you make for yourself."

Douglas MacArthur

"All of us have moments in our lives that test our courage."

Erma Bombeck

"Things are never so bad
they can't be made worse…
Everybody in Casablanca has problems.
Yours may work out."

Humphrey Bogart

"Difficulty need not foreshadow
despair or defeat.
Rather achievement can be
all the more satisfying
because of obstacles surmounted."

Judge William Hastie

"ONCE STRUGGLE IS GRASPED,
MIRACLES ARE POSSIBLE."

MAO TSE-TUNG

"Forgive yourself.

Make whatever corrections seem necessary.

Move on."

Peter Mc Williams

"An error doesn't become a mistake

until you refuse to correct it."

Orlando A. Battista

"LIFE **IS** WORTH LIVING."

Bishop Fulton Sheen

"I am living proof that we get second chances

and that the second time around is

BETTER than the first."

"This is the first day of the rest of your life.

LIVE STRONG

And GO FOR IT !"

Lance Armstrong

"There is no other way to survive
except to be in the moment.
Just as my accident and its aftermath
caused me to redefine what a hero is,
I had to take a hard look at what it means
to live as fully as possible in the present."

Christopher Reeve

"My parents taught me to believe in miracles.
My life is proof that they exist."

Jim Carrey

"A slip of the foot you may soon recover:
But a slip of the tongue - you may never get over!"

Benjamin Franklin

"About the time that I was dragging myself up from the depths,
I began to do a great deal of magazine illustration.
And I think it helped me to recover my self-confidence…"

Norman Rockwell

"If you cannot get rid of the family skeleton,

make it dance!"

George Bernard Shaw

*"People have to do what people have to do.
You have to be happy."*

Oksana Baiul

"I stayed in touch with who I was.
I didn't sell out. I didn't lose myself.
I didn't become someone else just for money.
I stayed me. I learned. I grew.
And I opened up some doors, or at least
showed some other people they can do it too.
I love the idea that there are people
who will be greater than me."

Queen Latifah

"If you're head gets too big,
it'll break your neck."

"It's now or never!"

Elvis

"Just fake it till you make it.
The prayers will seem phony,
but one day they'll become real,
and your faith will become real."

Bobby Kennedy

"Most people give up just when
they're about to achieve success."

H. Ross Perot

"A man is literally what he thinks!"

James Allen

"The difference between
the impossible and the possible
lies in a man's determination."

Tommy Lasorda

"Do not let what you cannot do
interfere with
what you CAN do."

John Wooden

"There is always room at the top."

Daniel Webster

"The mind is the limit.
As long as the mind can envision
the fact that you can do something,
You CAN do it-
as long as you really believe 100 percent."

Arnold Schwarzenegger

"Failure is only the opportunity
to more intelligently begin again."
Henry Ford

"Some men have thousands of reasons why they cannot do what they want to, when all they need is one reason they can."

Willis R. Whitney

"Do not wish to be anything but what you are, and try to be that perfectly."

St. Frances De Sales

"A man's as miserable as he thinks he is."

Lucius Annaeus Seneca

"The difference between
a successful person and others
is not a lack of strength,
not a lack of knowledge,
but rather in a lack of will."

Vincent T. Lombardi

"Unless you do something
BEYOND
what you have already mastered,
you will never grow."

Ralph Waldo Emerson

"In order to succeed,
we must first believe that we can."

Michael Korda

"Where I was born and
where and how I have lived
is unimportant.

It is what I have done
with where I have been
that should be of interest."

Dwight L. Moody

"The greatest thing in the world
is not so much where we are,
but in what direction
we are moving."

O. W. Holmes

"The worst bankrupt in the world

is the person

who has lost his enthusiasm."

H. W. Arnold

"NEVER,

NEVER, NEVER

QUIT."

Winston Churchill

"Whether you think you can

or think you can't-

you are right!"

Henry Ford

"You have a remarkable ability
which you never acknowledged before.
It is to look at a situation and
know whether you can do it.
And I mean really ***know*** the answer..."

Carl Frederick

"The first and most important step toward success

is the feeling that we CAN succeed."

Nelson Boswell

"Honesty is the first chapter
of the book of wisdom."

Thomas Jefferson

"Success doesn't come to you,
you go to it."

Marva Collins

*"Every situation, properly perceived,
becomes an opportunity."*

Helen Schucman

"A wise man will make
more opportunities
than he finds."

"The mould of a man's fortune
is in his hands."

Francis Bacon

"Opportunity rarely knocks on your door.
Knock rather on opportunity's door
if you ardently wish to enter."

B.C. Forbes

"Hold yourself responsible for a higher standard
than anybody else expects of you.
Never excuse yourself."

Henry Ward Beecher

"Life is what happens to you
while you are busy making other plans."

John Lennon

"Success...
seems to be connected with action.
Successful men keep moving.
They make mistakes,
but they don't quit."
Conrad Hilton

"In the middle of difficulty lies opportunity."

Albert Einstein

"Success seemed to be largely a matter of

hanging on after others have let go."

William Feather

"The only limit to our realization of tomorrow will be our doubts of today."

Franklin D. Roosevelt

"He who loses wealth loses much;
he who loses a friend loses more;
but he that loses courage loses all."
Cervantes

"If there are things you don't like
in the world you grew up in,
make your own life different."

Dave Thomas

"A successful man is one who
can lay a firm foundation with
the bricks that others throw at him."

Sidney Greenberg

**"A man is not finished when he is defeated.
He is finished when he quits."**

Richard Nixon

"Success is how HIGH you bounce

when you hit bottom."

General George Patton

"VICTORY

BELONGS TO

THE MOST PERSEVERING."

Napoleon

'It is never too late

to be who you might have been."

George Eliot

"I believe that everything you do BAD comes back to you."
Tupac Shakur

"IF YOU CAN'T STAND THE HEAT, GET OUT OF THE KITCHEN."
Harry S. Truman

"Life is 10% what you make it and 90% how you take it."
Irving Berlin

"Put all your eggs in one basket,

and then watch the basket."

Andrew Carnegie

"Get your advice from successful people.

Failures can only teach you how to fail."

David J. Schwartz

"USE NO DESCRIPTION

OF INTOXICATING DRINK."

P. T. BARNUM

"When one door closes, another door opens;
but we so often look so long and so
regretfully upon the closed door,
that we do not see the one
which opens for us."

Alexander Graham Bell

"Begin at the beginning
and go on
till you come to the end;
then Stop."

Lewis Carrol

"Even more people today have the means to live, but no meaning to live for."

Viktor Frankl

"The great question is not
whether you have failed,
but whether you are
content with failure."

William Shakespeare

"Sometimes even to live is an act of courage."

Lucius Annaeus Seneca

"What the mind of man can conceive
and believe,
the mind of man can achieve."

Napoleon Hill

"The only thing that stands between
a man and what he wants from life
is often merely the will to try it
and the faith to believe
that it is possible."

Richard M. DeVos

"Success is the maximum utilization
of the ability that you have."

Zig Ziglar

"Courage is resistance to fear,
mastery of fear,
not absence of fear."

Mark Twain

"Little minds attain and are subdued by misfortunes;
but great minds rise above them."

Washington Irving

"All things are difficult before they are easy."

Thomas Fuller

"Obstacles will look large
or small to you
according to whether you are large
or small."

"All men who have achieved
great things have been dreamers."

Orison Swett Marden

"Failure is success if we learn from it."

"When you cease to dream,

you cease to live."

Malcolm S. Forbes

"No one else could possibly be as vicious
to ourselves as we are.

Life really wants you to succeed.

In fact,
Life desperately NEEDS you to succeed."

Noah St. John

"No man ever achieved worth-while success
who did not, at one time or another,
find himself with at least one foot
hanging well over the brink of failure."

Napoleon Hill

"Don't be afraid to fail.
Don't waste energy trying to cover up failure.
Learn from your failures
and go on to the next challenge.
It's O.K.
If you're not failing,
you're not growing."

H. Stanley Judd

"We are not interested in the possibilities of defeat."

Queen Victoria

"Accept the challenges,
so that you may feel
the exhilaration of victory."

General George S. Patton

*"The future belongs
to those who believe
in the beauty of their dreams."*

Eleanor Roosevelt

"Genius is one percent inspiration

and ninety-nine percent perspiration."

"If there is a way to do it better…find it!"

Thomas Alva Edison

"Always do your best,
what you plant now, you will harvest later."

Og Mandino

"Everything can change in a Split Second."

David Baldacci

"To be what we are,
and to become what we are capable of becoming,
is the only end to life."

Robert Louis Stevenson

"All our dreams can come true-

if we have the courage to pursue them."

Walt Disney

"The greatest mistake a man can make

is to be afraid of making one."

Elbert Hubbard

"The successful man will profit from his mistakes,

and try again in a different way."

Dale Carnegie

"All difficult things have their origin in that which is easy

and great things in that which is small."

Lao-Tzu

"You need firm ground to stand on.

From there,

you can deal with that change."

Richard Nelson Bolles

"Ask, and it shall be given you;

Seek, and you shall find;

Knock, and it shall be opened to you.

For everyone who asks, receives;

And he who seeks, finds:

And to him who knocks,

it shall be opened."

Jesus

"Life didn't promise to be wonderful."

Teddy Pendergrass

"One may walk over the highest mountain

one step at a time."

Barbara Walters

"Keep working hard and

you can get anything that you want.

If God gave you the talent, you should go for it.

But don't think it's going to be easy. It's hard!"

Aaliyah

"Failure is the condiment
that gives success its flavor!"

Truman Capote

"The purpose of life is a life of purpose."

Robert Byrne

"Success is not measured
by what a man accomplished,
but by the opposition he has encountered
and the courage with which
he has maintained the struggle
against overwhelming odds."

Charles Lindbergh

"Focus on remedies, not on faults."

Jack Nicklaus

"IT IS A ROUGH ROAD
THAT LEADS TO THE
HEIGHTS OF GREATNESS."

Seneca

"If you're a champion,
you have to have it in your heart."

Chris Evert Lloyd

"If you really want something

you can figure out how to make it happen."

Cher Bono

"Have the courage to face a difficulty.

lest it kick you harder than you bargain for."

King Stanislaus I

"I have never been lost, but I will admit

to being confused for several weeks."

Daniel Boone

"You can't win unless you learn how to lose."

Kereem Abdul-Jabbar

"I have only one counsel for you-

BE MASTER."

Napoleon Bonaparte

"Seek not greatness but seek truth

and you will find both."

Horace Mann

"Have the courage to act instead of react."

Oliver Wendell Holmes

"Life is very interesting…
in the end, some of your greatest pains
become your greatest strengths."
Drew Barrymore

*"It is the sweet simple things of life
which are the real ones after all."*

Laura Ingalls Wilder

"Whatever you do,
do it with all your might.

Work at it early and late,
in season and out of season,
not leaving a stone unturned,
and never deferring
for a single hour
that which can be done
just as well now."

P. T. Barnum

"Don't look forward to the day you stop suffering,

because when it comes you'll know you're dead.

LUCK IS BELIEVING YOU'RE LUCKY."

Tennessee Williams

"About the time you can make ends meet,

somebody moves the ends."

Herbert Hoover

"Don't be afraid
to give up the GOOD
for the GREAT."

Kenny Rogers

"Courage is being afraid but going on anyway."

Dan Rather

"Apply yourself.
Get all the education you can,
but then, by God,

DO SOMETHING!

Don't just stand there,

MAKE IT HAPPEN."

Lee Iacocca

"A fool too late bewares

when all the peril is past."

Queen Elizabeth I

"IF YOU REST,

YOU RUST."

Helen Hayes

"If you wait,

all that happens is that you get older."

Mario Andretti

"GET BUSY LIVING

OR GET BUSY DYING."

Andy Dufresne

"My grandfather...taught me

to look up to people others looked down on

because we're not so different after all."

Bill Clinton

"When you lie down with dogs,
you get up with fleas."

Jean Harlow

"Don't worry.
Be happy."

Bobby McFerrin

"I believe that you can change.
I believe that you are not
what you have been,
but that you are
the possibility
of what you can be!"

Oprah Winfrey

"Never say never,
for if you live long enough, chances are
you will not be able to abide by its restrictions.
Never is a long undependable time
and life is too full of rich possibilities
to have restrictions placed upon it."

Gloria Swanson

"If at first you don't succeed;
Try, try again.
Then quit.
There's no use being a damn fool about it."
W. C. Fields

"I am concerned with the cracking up
that is happening all over..
I have tried to touch the feeling of people
who have self-propelled themselves in life
and have been successful in attaining something
they find they don't really want."
Elia Kazan

"I like the dreams of the future
better than the history of the past."
Thomas Jefferson

"Do what you can,
with what you have,
where you are."
Theodore Roosevelt

"The secret of success is
consistency of purpose."
Benjamin Disraeli

"Success is not a harbor but a voyage
with its own perils to the spirit.
The game of life is to come up a winner,
to be a success,
or to achieve what we set out to do.
Yet there is always a danger of failing as a human being.
The lesson most of us on this voyage never learn,
but can never quite forget,
is that to ***win***
is sometimes to ***lose***."

Richard M. Nixon

"The only disability in life is a bad attitude."

Scott Hamilton

"Giving up is the ultimate tragedy!"

Robert J. Donovan

"When you're down and out
something always turns up-
and it's usually
the noses of your friends."

Orson Welles

"The mass of men lead lives of quiet desperation."

Henry David Thoreau

"The longer I live
the more beautiful life becomes."

Frank Lloyd Wright

"Let there be spaces
in your togetherness."

Kahlil Gilbran

"By rights you're a king.
If I was you, I'd call for a new deal."

O. Henry

“Failure is impossible!”

Susan B. Anthony

“Gray skies are just clouds passing over.”

Frank Gifford

“Without deviation progress is not possible.”

Frank Zappa

"The state of your life
is nothing more than
a reflection of your state of mind."

Dr. Wayne W. Dyer

"Tomorrow is another day."

Scarlett O'Hara

"To be, or not to be: that is the question."

William Shakespeare

"Destiny is not a matter of chance,
it is a matter of choice;
it is not a thing to be waited for,
it is a thing to be achieved."

William Jennings Bryan

"People are always blaming their
circumstances for what they are.
I don't believe in circumstances.
The people who get on in this world
are the people who get up and look
for the circumstances they want
and, if they can't find them,
make them."

George Bernard Shaw

"To love oneself
is the beginning
of a lifelong romance."
Oscar Wilde

"Each person must live their life
as a role model for others."
ROSA PARKS

"There is no failure
except in no longer trying."
Elbert Hubbard

"Great emergencies and crises
show us how much greater our
vital resources are
than we had supposed."

William James

"You should examine yourself daily.

If you find faults,

You should correct them.

When you find none,

You should try even harder."

Xi Zhi

"Faced with the choice
between changing one's mind
and proving there is no need to do so,
almost everyone gets busy on the proof."

John Kenneth Galbraith

"If at first you don't succeed
you're running about average."

M. H. Anderson

"Even if you're on the right track,
you'll get run over if you just sit there."

Will Rogers

"The best thing about the future
is that it comes
only ONE day
at a time."

Abraham Lincoln

"I don't believe in instant fixes...
if we want to be true to ourselves
finding answers to the most important
questions of life is a process."

Christopher Reeve

"You must play BOLDLY to WIN."

Arnold Palmer

"It is common sense to take a method and try it.

If it fails, admit it frankly

and try another.

But above all, try something."

Franklin D. Roosevelt

"You gain strength, courage and confidence
by every experience
in which you really stop
to look fear in the face.
You are able to say to yourself,
'I lived through this horror.
I can take the next thing that comes along.'
You must do the thing you think you cannot do."

Eleanor Roosevelt

"Chance favors the prepared mind."
Louis Pasteur

"They say, 'Sticks and stones may break your bones,
but names will never hurt you.'
Personally, I prefer sticks and stones.
The wounds heal faster.

Fortunately I have learned to use selective deafness.
I now choose to hear only the encouraging words."

Guccione

"Mistakes are a fact of life.

It is the response to the error that counts."

Nikki Giovanni

"Reality is something you rise above."

Liza Minnelli

"Only by great risks can results be achieved."

Xerxes

"Be nice to people on your way up

because you meet them on your way down."

Jimmy Durante

"Have a very good reason for everything you do."

Sir Laurence Olivier

"IF IT WASN'T HARD,
EVERYONE WOULD DO IT.
IT'S THE **HARD**
THAT MAKES IT **GREAT**."

Tom Hanks

"Trying to grow up is hurting, you know.
You make mistakes.
You try to learn from them,
And when you don't,
It hurts even more."

Aretha Franklin

"Happiness is like a butterfly
which, when pursued
is always beyond our grasp
but, if you will sit down quietly,
may alight upon you."

Nathaniel Hawthorne

"SPEND SOME TIME ALONE EVERYDAY."

Dalai Lama

"Use a make-up table with everything close at hand

and don't rush,

otherwise you'll look like a patchwork quilt."

Lucille Ball

"NEVER, NEVER LISTEN TO ANYBODY THAT

TRIES TO DISCOURAGE YOU."

Mariah Carey

"Fain would I climb, yet fear I to fall."

Sir Walter Raleigh

"Luck, that's when preparation
and opportunity meet."

Pierre Elliot Trudeau

"Talent works, genius creates."

Robert Schumann

"IN THE END,

THE LOVE YOU TAKE

IS EQUAL TO

THE LOVE YOU MAKE."

Paul McCartney

"Set your goals high

And don't stop till you get there."

Bo Jackson

"Victory is not won in miles but in inches.

Win a little now,

hold your ground,

and later,

win a little more."

Louis L'Amour

"Obstacles don't have to stop you.

If you run into a wall,
don't turn around and give up.

Figure out how to climb it,
go through it or work around it.

I can accept failure but
I cannot accept not trying."

Michael Jordon

"Be not afraid,

but let your world

be lit by miracles."

Marianne Williamson

"If it weren't for caterpillars

there wouldn't be any butterflies."

Wess Roberts

"Dare something **WORTHY** !
Go for your dream.
You are the one
who can make a difference
in the world today!"

Dr. Joe Vitale

"Never say 'yes' to the first offer,
No matter how good it looks!"

Roger Dawson

"If you live long enough, you're bound to encounter some rough storms. No one is immune to tragedy in this life. The house is the same, the storm is the same, but what makes the difference is the foundation. The question each of us must answer, sooner or later, is this: How secure is the foundation on which I'm building my life?"

Lisa Beamer

"The difficult we do immediately, the impossible takes a little longer."

The U.S. Army Corp. of Engineers

"Never take rejection personally."

Thomas J. Stanley, M.D.

"Trust the Divine Power within you
and you will find that
this inner Presence and Power
will lift you up,
heal you
and inspire you
and set you on the high road to happiness,
serenity, and the fruition of your ideals."

John Murphy

"I always entertain great hopes."

Robert Frost

"Making a mistake is no excuse for living as a mistake."

Mamie McCollough

"HERE IS A TEST
TO FIND WHETHER
YOUR MISSION ON EARTH
IS FINISHED:

IF YOU'RE ALIVE, IT ISN'T."

Richard Bach

"Good old-fashioned common sense

has always been a mighty rare commodity."

John D. Rockefeller

"Focus on the POSITIVE."

Matthew McKay

"As soon as you trust yourself,

you will know how to live."

Johann Wolfgang von Goethe

"Nothing is, unless our thinking makes it so."

William Shakespeare

"TRANSFORM YOUR INNER CRITIC."

John Gray, Ph.D.

"A man can make mistakes,

but only an idiot

persists in his error."

Cicero

"God does not command

that we do great things,

only little things

with great love."

Mother Teresa

"Believe that life is worth living,

and your belief will help create that fact."

William James

"SUCCESS DOES NOT COME EASY."

Mike Ditka

"It's okay to say NO!"

Gerald R. Ford

"Don't be afraid to fail-

the only time you HAVE TO succeed

is the last time you try!"

Phillip H. Knight

"DO THE RIGHT THING."

Abraham Lincoln Marovitz

"The harder you work to succeed-
the harder it is to fail."

Coach Ray Meyer

"To find yourself,
THINK for yourself."

Socrates

"Sometimes you have to take

intensive measures

to prove them wrong."

Patrick Swayze

"Accidents are seldom the answers.

GOOD BREAKS count most

in what they lead to-

IF we follow through."

Alex Osborn

"NEVER SAY DIE. NEVER BE SATISFIED."

Orville Redenbacher

"If you do not change,

you can become extinct."

Spencer Johnson, M.D.

"Do it yourself!"

Lawrence Welk

"Experience is not what happens to a man;
it is what a man does
with what happens to him."

Aldous Huxley

"Clear your mind…
of the clutter of the negative things that have happened to you.
The negative experiences of the past stand like cloudbanks
between you and your psychic mind and your conscious mind.
You cannot receive divine guidance when you labor
under the emotion of fear, hatred and anxiety."

Norvell

"Lots of people don't know where to start.

...It's your life. Go with your gut."

Maria Shriver

"There is nothing to fear but fear itself."

Franklin Delano Roosevelt

"I HAVE A DREAM..."

Martin Luther King

"...There really is such a thing as 'mind over matter,'
and ... the principle can enable one
to disregard present pain
in the hope of future gain."

Rose Fitzgerald Kennedy

"Miracles happen
to those who believe in them."

Bernard Berenson

"No matter what happens,

DO NOT PANIC.

The panic stricken individual

cannot think or act

effectively."

J. Paul Getty

"They CAN
because
they think they can."
Virgil

*"We take life for granted
until a crisis wakes us up...
Crisis is the* MIRROR
of PURPOSE."
Richard J. Leider

"The world we live in
is the world we choose to live in,
whether, consciously or unconsciously.

If we choose bliss,
that is what we get.

If we choose misery,
we get that too."

Anthony Robbins

"No one is "DOOMED" to bad luck."

Napoleon Hill

"Your body has a remarkable capacity
to heal itself and
do so more quickly
than we ever thought possible.

...Ask your inner wisdom
what it is that you need to do to heal."

Dr. Dean Ornish

"I had to pick myself up
and get on with it.

Do it all over again,
only even better this time!"

Sam Walton

"THOSE WHO DARE

TO FAIL MISERABLY

CAN ACHIEIVE GREATLY."

John F. Kennedy

"A GOOD HEAD

AND A GOOD HEART

ARE ALWAYS

A FORMDABLE COMBINATION."

Nelson Mandela

"I want you to
LISTEN to what
your conscious commands you to do
and to go on to carry it out
to the best of your knowledge.

Then will you live to see
that in the long run-
in the long-run I say!-
SUCCESS WILL FOLLOW YOU
precisely because
you had forgotten to think about it!"

Viktor Frankl

"Hold your head high,

stick your chest out.

YOU CAN MAKE IT.

It gets dark sometimes

But morning comes..."

"KEEP HOPE ALIVE."

Jesse Jackson

"Just go out there and
DO
what you have to do."

Martina Navratilova

"The man who does things makes mistakes,

but he never makes the biggest mistake of all-

doing nothing."

Benjamin Franklin

"I learned that if
you want to make it bad enough,
no matter how bad it is,
you can make it."

Gayle Sayers

"In oneself lies the whole world
and if you know how to look and learn,
the door is there and the key is in your hand.

Nobody on earth can give you
either the key or the door to open,
except yourself."

Jiddu Krishnamurti

"Know your lines and

don't bump into the furniture."

Spencer Tracy

"BE NOT SIMPLY GOOD -

BE GOOD FOR SOMETHING."

Henry David Thoreau

"... Use the experience of suffering
as a doorway for change!"

Dr. Dean Ornish

"If you want to cut your own throat, don't come to me for a bandage."
"You may have to fight a battle more than once to win it."

Margaret Thatcher

"It is during our darkest moments that we must focus to see the light."

Aristotle Onassis

"To design the future effectively,

you must first let go of your past."

Charles J. Givens

"Push yourself,
again & again.
Don't give an inch
until the final buzzer sounds."

Larry Bird

"Talent alone won't make you a success,

neither will

being in the right place at the right time:

UNLESS YOU ARE READY.

The most important questions is-

ARE YOU READY?"

Johnny Carson

"When it comes to LUCK,

make your own."

Bruce Springsteen

"Winners never quit

and quitters never win."

Ted Turner

"Let us DO or DIE."

Warren Buffet

"Success is the sum of details."

Harvey S. Firestone

"So many of our dreams
at first seem impossible-
then they seem improbable-
and then, when we summon the will
they soon become inevitable."

Christopher Reeve

"A **BIG** man has no time to do anything
but just sit and be **BIG**."

"NEVER CONFUSE A SINGLE DEFEAT
WITH A FINAL DEFEAT."

F. Scott Fitzgerald

"Everything you need,
you already have.
You are complete right now.

You are a whole total person,
not an apprentice person
on the way to someplace else.

Your completeness must be
understood by you
and experienced in your thoughts
as your own personal reality."

Beverly Sills

"He is able who thinks he is able."

Buddha

"We choose what attitudes

we have right now.

And it's a continuing choice."

John Maxwell

"We are all proud of making little mistakes.

It gives us the feeling we don't make any big ones."

Andy Rooney

"Allow yourself to

"DREAM BIG DREAMS"

...and remember

FAILURE IS NOT

AN OPTION."

Brian Tracy

"It's important to give it all you have
while you have the chance."

Shania Twain

"Look to the future,
because that's where you'll spend
the rest of your life."

"Don't stay in bed,
unless you can make money in bed."

George Burns

" When there is a start to be made

don't step over!

Start where you are."

Edgar Cayce

"I never doubted my ability,

but when you hear all your life you're inferior,

it makes you wonder. . . "

Hank Aaron

"Look, I don't want to wax philosophic

but I will say that

if you're alive,

you've got to flap your arms and legs,

you've got to jump around a lot,

for life is the very opposite of death

and therefore you must

at the very least

think noisy and colorfully

or you're not alive."

Mel Brooks

"To state "we have problems'

is not particularly helpful...

Do Something

-ANYTHING-

Just DO Something."

Thomas A. Harris

"Give 'em Hell !"

Harry S. Truman

"As long as you're going to be thinking anyway,

THINK BIG."

Donald Trump

"Drag your thoughts
away from your troubles...
by the ears, by the heals,
or any other way you can manage it."

"It ain't what you don't know
that gets you into trouble,
it's what you know for sure
that just ain't so."

Mark Twain

"I'm a survivor - a living example of what people can go through and still survive."

Elizabeth Taylor

"The person interested in success has to learn to view failure as a healthy, inevitable part of the process of getting to the top."

Dr. Joyce Brothers

"When you have a dream,

you've got to grab it

and never let go."

Carol Burnett

"Don't compromise yourself.

You are all you've got."

Janis Joplin

"We should never let
our fears hold us back
from pursuing hopes."

John F. Kennedy

"There are no hopeless situations;
there are only men who have grown
hopeless about them."

Clare Booth Luce

"We must accept

finite disappointment,

but we must never lose

infinite hope."

Martin Luther King

"If you WILL IT, it is NO dream."

Theodore Herzl

"All things are possible

until

they are proven impossible-

and even the impossible

may only be so,

as of now."

Pearl Buck

"Man is not made for defeat.

A man can be destroyed

but not defeated."

Ernest Hemingway

"Nobody ever drowned in his own sweat."

Ann Landers

"Remember,
a dead fish can float downstream
but it takes a live one to swim upstream."

W. C. Fields

"We all have big changes in our lives
that are more or less a second chance."

Harrison Ford

"SOMETIMES I LIE AWAKE AT NIGHT

AND ASK WHY ME?

Then a voice answers and says:

'Nothing personal,

your name just happened to come up.' "

Charles M. Schultz

"Don't spend time beating on a wall,

hoping to transform it into a door."

Coco Chanel

"It's a damned long, boggy, dangerous way…"

"Our greatest glory consists not in never failing

but in rising every time we fall."

Oliver Goldsmith

"He who has courage and faith will never perish in misery."

"Everyone has inside of him a piece of good news.

The good news is that you don't know how great you can be!"

Anne Frank

"Everyone's got it in him,
if he'll only make up his mind
and stick at it."

Charles Schwab

"Setting a goal is not just the main thing.
It is deciding how you will go about achieving it
and *staying* with that plan."

Tom Landry

"Do not anticipate trouble
or worry about
what may never happen.

Keep in the sunlight.

Do not fear mistakes.
You will know failure.
Continue to reach out.

When in doubt, don't.

When you're finished changing,
you're finished."

Ben Franklin

"Normal is in the eye of the beholder."

Whoopi Goldberg

"There is no greater agony than

bearing an untold story inside you.'

Maya Angelou

"For what is a man, what has he got?
If not himself, then he has naught."

Paul Anka

"Success is a lousy teacher.
It seduces smart people
into thinking they can't lose."

Bill Gates

"There have been times

when I deliberately tried to take my life...

I think I must have been crying out

for some attention."

Judy Garland

"YOU MISS 100% OF THE SHOTS

YOU NEVER TAKE."

Wayne Gretsky

"Regret and recriminations

only hurt your soul."

Armand Hammer

"I dwell in possibility."

Emily Dickinson

"I tell you the past is a bucket of ashes."

Carl Sandburg

"Storms make trees take deeper roots."

Dolly Parton

"Few men during their lifetime
come anywhere near exhausting
the resources dwelling within them.
There are deeper wells of strength
that are never used."

Richard E. Byrd

"It is important to stay passionate."

Nicolas Cage

"The roughest road often leads to the top."

Christina Aguilera

"Ya gotta have a dream.

If ya don't have a dream,

how ya gonna make a dream come true?"

Oscar Hammerstein

"Have a good cry,

wash out your heart.

If you keep it inside

it'll tear you apart."

Dr. Hook

"A HUNCH IS CREATIVITY

TRYING TO TELL YOU

SOMETHING."

Frank Capra

"I can never decide whether my dreams
are the result of my thoughts or
my thoughts the result of my dreams."

D. H. Lawrence

"Be who you are and say what you feel,
because those who mind don't matter
and those who matter don't mind."

Dr. Seuss

"If you have it and
you know you have it,
then you have it!

If you have it
and don't know you have it,
you don't have it!

If you don't have it
but you *think* you have it,
then you have it!"

"How sweet *it* is!"

Jackie Gleason

"Those who don't know how to
weep with their whole heart,
don't know how to laugh either."

Golda Meir

"There's always someone to tell you 'you have to.'
Wrong. Don't!
Rather, spend time finding out who you really are.
Work on being more of that."

Shirley Jones

"A lot of people are afraid
to say what they want.
That's why they don't ***get*** what they want."

Madonna

"Happiness isn't getting what you want,
it's wanting what you got."

Garth Brooks

"I do my best work when I'm in pain and turmoil."

STING

"IF YOU"RE GOING THROUGH *HELL*,

KEEP GOING!"

Walt Disney

"Some men see things as they are and say "Why?"

I dream things that never were, and say, "Why not?"

George Bernard Shaw

"We build too many walls
and not enough bridges."

Sir Isaac Newton

"So tonight you better stop

and rebuild all your ruins,

because peace and trust can win the day

despite of all your losing."

Led Zeppelin

"YOU'RE ONLY GIVEN

A LITTLE SPARK OF MADNESS.

YOU MUSTN'T LOSE IT."

ROBIN WILLIAMS

"Avoid having your ego so close to your position

that when your position falls,

you're ego goes with it."

Colin Powell

"The only place where

success come before *work*

is in a dictionary."

Vidal Sassoon

"Slow down and enjoy life.

It's not only the scenery you miss

by going too fast-

you also miss the sense of where you are going

and *why*."

Eddie Cantor

"Be like a duck,

calm on the surface,

but always paddling like the dickens underneath."

Michael Caine

"The greatest glory never comes from falling,

but from rising each time you fall."

Clay Aiken

"Review priorities and ask the question:

What is the best use of our time right now?

Failing to plan is planning to fail."

Alan Lakein

"Sometimes we are forced in directions
that we ought to have found for ourselves…

What we DO does not define who we are.

What defines us is
how well we rise after falling."

Lionel Bloch

"You may have a fresh start
any moment you choose,
for this thing we call "failure"
is not the falling down,
but the staying down."

Mary Pickford

"Do not wait:
The time will never be "just right".
Start where you stand, and work
with whatever tools you may have
at your command, and better tools
will be found as you go along.."

Napoleon Hill

"Your heartsong is your inner beauty.
It's the song in your heart
that wants you to help
make yourself be a better person,
and to help other people do the same.
Everybody has one."

"If you believe in magical, musical hearts,
and if you believe you can be happy,
then you, too, will hear your song."

Mattie Stepanek

"Give your dreams the wings to fly.
You have everything you need
if you JUST BELIEVE !"

Josh Groban

"You got to know when to hold them,
know when to fold them,
know when to walk away,
and know when to run."

Kenny Rogers

"I think luck is the sense to recognize an opportunity
and the ability to take advantage of it.
Everyone has bad breaks,
but everyone also has opportunities.
The man that can smile at his breaks
and grab his chances gets on."

Samuel Goldwyn

"Life is about two things-
Loving and Learning.
You learn so-o much from things
when they go wrong."

Jennifer Lopez

"Every time you have a breakdown,

it is just to get to a new paradigm."

"Hear your own voice

and you will find your way."

Susan Sarandon

"Step into the *Outer Limits.*

If you want a better life than which you now have,

you must learn to overcome that natural fear

and to step outside what has become

comfortable and familiar."

Stedman Graham

"Recognize all the parts that make the whole,

For YOU are the maker."

Shirley MacLaine

"Don't be afraid to take a big step if one is indicated.
You can't cross a chasm in two small jumps."

DAVID LLOYD GEORGE

"Most things are done by choice...

Choice produces results,

but it's up to you to choose what you want."

Catherine Ponder

"I think gravity sets into everything,
including careers,
but pendulums DO swing
and mountains DO become valleys
after a while... **IF** you keep on walking."

Sylvester Stallone

No problem can withstand

the assault of sustained thinking."

Voltaire

"We come. We go.

And in between we try to understand."

Rod Steiger

"I have been impressed with
the urgency of doing.

Knowing is not enough;
we must apply.

Being willing is not enough;
WE MUST DO."

Leonardo da Vinci

"Aim for the moon.

If you miss

you may hit a star."

W. Clement Stone

"The future is always beginning NOW."

Mark Strand

"If you act like you know what you are doing,
you can do anything you want-
except neurosurgery."

Sharon Stone

"You must try to generate
happiness within yourself.
If you aren't happy in one place,
chances are you won't be happy
anyplace!"

Ernie Banks

"The past just came up and kicked me,

(but)

Success is the sweetest revenge!"

Vanessa Williams

"A problem is a chance

for you to do your BEST!"

Duke Ellington

"The greater danger,

for most of us,

lies not in setting our aim too high

and falling short;

but in setting our aim too low,

and achieving our mark."

Michelangelo

"Great things are done

by a series of small things

brought together."

Vincent Van Gogh

"Nothing is more intolerable
than to have to admit
to yourself
your own errors."

Ludwig von Beethoven

"The most effective way to do it,

is to DO it."

Amelia Earhart

"Turn your wounds into wisdom."

Oprah

"Invent a PAST from the PRESENT."

Daniel Stern

"It's going to be unbelievable, you know.

There's going to be a lot of people cheering...

And, hey, we'll see how it goes."

Sammy Sosa

"A champion is
someone who gets up
when he can't."

Jack Dempsey

"It takes courage
to grow up
and become
who you really are."

e e cummings

"If they can make

penicillin

out of moldy bread,

they can sure make

SOMETHING

out of you!"

Muhammad Ali

"They always say time changes things,

but actually

you have to CHANGE them yourself."

Andy Warhol

"**ACTION**

is the foundational key

to all **SUCCESS!**"

Pablo Picasso

"The gods help them that help themselves."

Aesop

"Worry is the interest paid

to those who borrow trouble."

George Washington

"I've never seen a monument erected to a pessimist."

Paul Harvey

"Have no fear of moving into the unknown.

Simply step out fearlessly,

knowing that I am with you,

therefore no harm can befall you.

All is very, very well.

Do this in complete faith and confidence."

Pope John Paul II

"Courage is being

SCARED TO DEATH...

and saddling up anyway."

John Wayne

"If you fell down yesterday, stand up today."

H. G. Wells

"So WHAT! Do IT ANYWAY!"

"Take action. Keep on keepin' on!"

Jack Canfield

"How very little can be done

under the spirit of fear."

Florence Nightingale

"I don't know what the future may hold,

but I know who holds the future."

Ralph Abernathy

"In wisdom gathered over time
I have found that every experience
is a form of exploration."

Ansel Adams

*"You only live once,
but if you do it right,
once is enough!"*

Mae West

"It's the moment you think you can't

that you realize you can!"

Celine Dion

"A pessimist sees

the difficulty in every opportunity.

An optimist sees

the opportunity in every difficulty."

Winston Churchill

"Dream as if

You'll live FOREVER."

James Dean

"Do you wish to be great?

Then begin by being."

St. Augustine

"You'll never find yourself
until you face the truth."
Pearl Bailey

"Judge each day not by the harvest you reap,
but by the seeds you plant."
Robert Louis Stevenson

"Eighty percent of success is showing up."
Woody Allen

"Ya gots to work with
what you gots to work with."

Stevie Wonder

"When in Rome, do as the Romans.
Adjust your style.
Develop more adaptability."

Dr. Tony Alessandra

"Before you can win,
you have to believe you are worthy."

Mike Ditka

"Action is the antidote to despair."

Joan Baez

'The trouble is that

everyone talks about reforming others

and no one thinks about reforming himself."

St. Peter of Alcantara

"Remember tonight,

for it is the beginning of always."

Dante Alighieri

"You can turn painful situations around

through laughter.

If you can find humor in anything,

you can survive it."

Bill Cosby

"It's kind of fun

to do the impossible."

Walt Disney

"It's best to have failure happen early in life.

It wakes up the Phoenix bird in you

so you rise from the ashes."

Anne Baxter

"Be always sure you're right,

then go ahead."

Davy Crockett

"NOBODY

who ever gave his BEST

regretted it."

George Halas

"RULE YOUR MIND

OR IT WILL RULE YOU."

HORACE

"This will never happen to me again.

One day we're gonna laugh at this."

Nadja Piatka

"Don't dwell on what went wrong.

Instead, focus on what to do next.

Spend your energies on moving forward,

toward finding the answer."

Denis Waitley

"Turn lemons into lemonade."

Wally "Famous" Amos

"If you can keep your head
when all about you are losing theirs
and blaming it on you,
. . .you'll be a Man, my son!"

Rudyard Kipling

"There is no substitution for paying attention."

Diane Sawyer

"Stand up and go,
your faith has saved you."
Jesus Christ

"Just don't give up trying to do
what you really want to do.
Where there is love and inspiration,
I don't think you can go wrong."

Ella Fitzgerald

"Get rid of the garbage in your life."

Dave Pelzer

"Tomorrow is a mystery and today is a gift.

That is why we call it the present."

Cherie Carter-Scott Ph.D.

"It's a nice day to start again."

"Pick it up."

Billy Joel

"Inside of us, a champion is waiting,

ready to rise and radically transform

every aspect of our existence."

Jack M. Zufelt

"Our worst fear is not that we are inadequate.
Our deepest fear is that we are powerful beyond measure.
It is our light, not our darkness, that most frightens us.
We ask ourselves,
who I am to be brilliant, gorgeous, talented and fabulous?

Actually, who are you not to be?
You are a child of God.
Your playing small does not serve the world.

As we let our own light shine,
we unconsciously give other people
permission to do the same.

As we are liberated from our fear,
our presence automatically liberates others."

Nelson Mandela

"If we keep doing what we're doing,
we're going to keep getting
what we're getting."

Stephen R. Covey

"Change the changeable,
accept the unchangeable,
and remove yourself
from the unacceptable."

Denis Waitley

"If you believe it, you can live it.
I know that to be true…
Everybody told me, "You won't make it.
You're too tough, you're too heavy,
you're too this, you're too that."

I always thought in my head,
"Mmmm, no, you're wrong."
I wouldn't argue with people;
I just believed in myself and kept going.

I don't know where I got that,
who instilled it in me,
but it definitely guided me
through the rocky waters of show biz."

Rosie O'Donnell

"The quotations
when engraved upon the memory
give you good thoughts.
They also make you anxious
to read the authors
and look for more."

Sir Winston Churchill

"Poetry, biographies and all the other
great books will greatly enrich your life.
Drink deeply from those great books
of your own choosing and
you will enrich yourself."

Coach John Wooden

"Down every dark corridor
there is a door somewhere
that will open to the Light.
...There IS hope!"

Dana Reeve

"There shall be joy in the morning."
"Make it happen!"

Mariah Carey

"You are such a messenger!
Keep on deciding what you want to become
in the next highest version of yourself…
Keep on working toward that!
Keep on! Keep on!
This is God Work we're up to, you & I…
So KEEP ON!!!!!

Neale Donald Walsch

"Are you ready?
Okay.
Let's roll."

Todd Beamer

Picking up the Pieces

Exercising Your Choice

PICKING UP THE BEST

"You can pick up the best" said the voice.

"You can leave all the rest, it's your choice."

In order to pick up the best, you will need to take inventory. Use this list to indicate what you see in "your pieces." They may be broken but they are still there. Check them off to "pick them up." Picking them up is acknowledging that they are yours. Read each item slowly and carefully. Check the box if you see even a trace of this quality within yourself.

Acknowledge each with a blink or a nod or some other physical action.

This will be the equivalent to "saving" the item in your data base.

Come back later and do it again to see if you missed any.

Repeat and review this exercise as often as needed.

Do it several times a day if necessary.

☐ Optimism

I see the glass half full (most of the time).

☐ Inspiration

I am inspired by great success stories of others.

☐ Truth

All that I am is firmly based upon that which is true.

☐ Character

I have good moral strength. I know right from wrong.

☐ Motivation

I know what I want and I can get up and get it.

☐ Perseverance

I am determined to keep on going until I get there.

☐ Communication

I am able to say what I mean and express what I want.

☐ Challenge

I can step up and give my best when necessary.

☐ Dignity

I recognize and respect the worth of my "self".

☐ Blessings

I recognize that I am greatly blessed with many gifts.

☐ Respect

I respect myself and am capable of respecting others.

☐ Strength

I have an incredible inner ability to endure and triumph.

☐ Energy

I have a storehouse of unlimited energy at my core.

☐ Support

I have a planned system in place which can provide support for me when the load gets too heavy.

☐ Compassion

I have acknowledged the pain. I am willing to release it.

☐ Love

I am aware of the many forms of love. I am willing to allow myself to participate, both in giving and receiving.

☐ Joy

I am capable of joy. I deserve intense happiness.

☐ Laughter

I find humor in every day occurrences.
I allow myself to smile and to laugh.

☐ Rapture

I remember blissful ecstatic happiness.
I willingly return there again and again.

☐ Vitality

I am pleased and very excited at the thought of being alive right now.

☐ Intelligence

I am intelligent and knowledgeable.
I have drawn wisdom from this experience.

☐ Imagination

I vividly create mental visions of what I want my life to look like.
I engage all of my senses in each experience.

☐ Kind- spirited

I am a caring person who genuinely desires the best for others as well as for myself.

☐ Friendship

People are pleased to have me for a friend.

☐ Gratitude

I am appreciative of the blessings in my life.
I readily express these feelings of gratitude.

☐ Wisdom

I have both knowledge AND experience.
Book sense + street smart = wisdom.

☐ Courage

I have looked danger in the face and I have survived.
I am free of fear.

☐ Appreciation

I am aware of and I am sensitive to many things in my life. I graciously appreciate and acknowledge them.

☐ Potential

I have fabulous possibilities within me waiting to emerge and flourish. I know in my heart that this is true.

☐ Possibilities

I am like an apple ***seed*** which can grow into a full and bountiful ***tree*** giving ***bushels*** of apples.

☐ Dreams

My head is full of visions, ideas, thoughts and concepts waiting to manifest. I am often busy "dreaming".

☐ Hope

My heart recognizes my dreams and says "YES!" to them.

☐ Pride

I can stand up and brush myself off.
It will not hurt my ego.

☐ Health

I firmly believe that I can restore my well-being and my physical health through my actions and my attitude.

☐ Wishes

I have launched many desires and yearnings which are still in orbit. I do believe that the best is yet to come.

☐ Dedication

I am devoted to that which is inscribed upon my being.

☐ Curiosity

I have an inquisitive nature which leads me to explore other options and endless possibilities.

☐ Awe

I have an overwhelming respect and reverence for that which amazes me.

☐ Cheer

I am delightfully encouraged. The game is not over. There is still hope.

☐ Enthusiasm

I have an intense feeling of encouragement about me. This is good.

☐ Devotion

I am seriously dedicated to my purpose.
I am steadfast in my belief.

☐ Accomplishments

I have a long list of past successes upon which to base my expectations.

☐ Achievements

I have already accomplished many other feats.
This is just one more to do.

☐ Determination

It is not a matter of ***whether*** I will make it, but rather it is a matter of ***when*** I will make it.

☐ Concentration

I have a high-intensity laser-quality focus.
I can burn through this rather quickly.

☐ Abundance

There is an unlimited supply of riches which comes to me precisely as needed.

☐ Peace

There is a calm and quiet freedom which empowers me.
It restores and refreshes my spirit.

☐ Knowledgeable

I am well-informed but I constantly seek to learn more.
I am continuing my education.

☐ Independent

If it is meant to be, it is up to me.
I am totally responsible.

☐ Conscientious

I have been thorough and attentive to the details.
It is right and good for me.

☐ Self-reliant

I myself have everything that is necessary.
I am not a "half." I am whole.

☐ Competent

I am fully capable and legally authorized to attain that which I seek.

☐ Confident

I CAN and I WILL fully accomplish my goal.
There are only possibilities.

☐ Dynamic

I am bursting with exuberance.
I am anxious to get started.

☐ Hard-working

I am ready and willing to do whatever it takes to change my current situation.

☐ Creative

I have a vivid imagination and an inventive spirit.
I am unique.

☐ Artistic

I create beauty in places that once were plain or ordinary.

☐ Unique

I am unlike any other. I am truly unique.

☐ Prompt

Most of the time, I am on time.
I am aware that showing up is often half of the battle.

☐ Positive

I see the bright side of things, even now.
I am an optimist.

☐ Outgoing

I am a cordial and pleasant.
I am comfortable socializing with others.

☐ Responsible

I am accountable for myself. I know right from wrong.
I recognize that there are consequences for all actions.

☐ Friendly

I make friends easily. I am likable.
People enjoy being with me.

☐ Entertaining

I often make people laugh.
People find me amusing and talented.

☐ Responsive

I am sensitive to and perceptive of those around me.

☐ Expressive

I am careful in my choice of words and of my actions.
I mean what I say. I am aware of my body language.

☐ Negotiator

I am tactful at bargaining.
I often get others to agree to compromise.

☐ Flexible

I have been known to bend without breaking.
I am willing to do so now.

☐ Accepting

I am willing take this on.
It is not a burden. It is a challenge.

☐ Open-minded

I am open to suggestions. Change is good.
I will consider other options.

☐ Warm-hearted

I am tender, appreciative and understanding of others.
This has not made me bitter.

☐ Relaxed

I am free of tension. I am not uptight.
I know how to let go.

☐ Likable

I am a warm and friendly person.
People like to be around me.

☐ Instinct

I have a natural inborn prompting mechanism within me.
It is available to guide me when needed.

☐ Vision

I have a clear picture of a better situation.
I am able to bring it into focus.
I can zoom in to the details of what it looks like.

☐ Clarity

The vision is complete with all of the intricate details.
I can see it clearly now.

☐ Patience

I want it all. I want it now but I respect the necessary gestation period for it to be.

☐ Reasonable

It is logical and reasonable to believe I can have this.
It is within the scope of "if".

☐ Assertive

I have presented my claim. I have laid out my demands.
I claim it as mine.

☐ Generosity

I willingly share my abundance with a charitable heart.

☐ Purpose

I have a purpose to fulfill. I am not done yet.

☐ Healing

I have the ability to restore and renew myself.
I can help in the healing process.

☐ Empowered

I draw my strength from a Higher Power.
It is the Source of my being.

☐ Protected

I am thereby protected. No harm can come to me.

☐ Faith

I sincerely believe without a doubt that it shall be!

☐ I **am** picking up the best.

☐ I **am** leaving all the rest.

LEAVING ALL REST

"You can pick up the best" said the voice.

"You can leave all the rest, it's your choice."

The best time to throw out the trash is when you are cleaning up. In order to "leave all the rest" once again you will need to take inventory. This time you will need to be a bit more demonstrative. Photocopy these next pages for your own personal use. Use this list to indicate what want **to eliminate** in your life.

For the purpose of this exercise you have the author's permission to copy the following pages (pg. 256 & 257). Use the copied pages for the following exercise. Circle the items if you see them in your broken pieces.

If the item that bothers you is not listed here, write it in yourself. Now cross off your "trash" with a big black marker to eliminate or delete it.

Hold the paper at arms length and observe all of the black mark deletions. Now crumble up the paper as tightly as possible. Throw it on the floor and stomp on it, again and again and again. Tear it to pieces if you'd like. Flush it, burn it or whatever. Notice and acknowledge how this makes you feel. Acknowledge with a blink, a nod, a "yes!" or some other physical action. This will serve as an acknowledgement which is equivalent to "saving" the deletion in your data base. Repeat and review this exercise as often as possible. Keep repeating this exercise until you have nothing left to circle or delete. Passionately enjoy this deletion exercise. Consider your problem permanently deleted and act accordingly.

Self-Pity	**Pessimism**	**Strife**
Sadness	**Heartache**	**Sorrow**
Fatigue	**Nervousness**	**Depression**
Crisis	**Drama**	**Nightmares**
Insomnia	**Apathy**	**Doubt**
Gloom	**Despair**	**Blame**
Misery	**Disgrace**	**Adversity**
Embarrassment	**Helplessness**	**Vulnerability**
Jealousy	**Mistrust**	**Suspicious**
Lack	**Scarcity**	**Poverty**
Pain	**Suffering**	**Illness**
Anxiety	**Overwhelmed**	**Exhaustion**
Anger	**Argumentative**	**Sarcasm**
Grief	**Guilt**	**Rejection**
Alcoholism	**Addiction**	**Dependency**
Unworthy	**Lack of confidence**	**Insecurity**

Limitations	**Disabilities**	**Handicaps**
Fearful	**Frail**	**Fragile**
Hopeless	**Sad**	**Moody**
Broke	**Bankrupt**	**Struggling**
Delayed	**Lateness**	**Unmotivated**
Ignored	**Forgotten**	**Despondent**
Temptation	**Lust**	**Sin**
Selfishness	**Corruption**	**Greed**
Foolishness	**Sarcasm**	**Sulking**
Irritable	**Judgmental**	**Bad-Tempered**
Laziness	**Illogical**	**Unreasonable**
Pride	**Arrogant**	**Conceited**
Grumpy	**Dull**	**Bored**
Envy	**Defiance**	**Hate**
Overindulgence	**Gluttony**	**Demanding**

Something worst than anything listed here

Annotated Index

By their words, we are inspired.

Listen carefully
so that you may hear,
for such is the Power of Choice.

We hereby, in this *book of quotations*, would like to graciously acknowledge and thereby give credit to the many contributors who have inadvertently, through their "encouraging words", lent their experience and wisdom to countless others who seek to follow in the Pursuit of Happiness. It is by their words and their example that many lives have been enriched. Many more will follow.

Aaliyah (1979-2001). American rhythm & blues singer, **91**

Aaron, Hank (1934-). Baseball player, member of U. S. Baseball Hall of Fame, **160**

Abdul-Jabbar, Kareem (1947-). NBA Basketball athlete, **95**

Abernathy, Ralph (1936-1996). American civil rights leader, **211**

Adams, Ansel (1902-1984). Renowned photographer, **212**

Aesop (620-560 BC). Greek writer renowned for his *Fables*, **208**

Aiken, Clay (1978-). Singer, famed second place winner of American Idol, **189**

Aguilera, Christina (1980-) American pop singer, Mouseketeer, survivor of abuse, ridicule and ostracism, **179**

Alessandra, Tony – Author of The Platinum Rule (1998), **216**

Ali, Muhammad (1942-) born as Cassius Marcellus Clay, Jr. American boxer, **206**

Alighieri, Dante (1265-1321). Poet., author of *Divine Comedy* and *The Inferno*, **217**

Allen, James (1864-1912) Author of *As A Man Thinketh*, **62**

Allen, Woody (1935-). Actor, comedian, **215**

Amos, Wally "Famous" Founder of Famous Amos Cookies and the Uncle Noname Company, created an entrepreneurial empire, lost it and recreated another. Author of *The Power in You*, **222**

Anderson, M. (1888-1959). Dramatist, called one of the most important playwrights of the early twentieth century, Pulitzer Prize winner, author of *Key Largo* and *All's Quiet on the Western Front*, **113**

Andretti, Mario (1940-). American race car driver, Formula One World Champion, **100**

Angelou, Maya (1928-). American poet and author of *I Know Why the Caged Bird Sings* (1970), voice for civil rights activism in America, **174**

Anka, Paul (1941-). Canadian singer, songwriter, **175**

Anthony, Susan B. (1820-1906). Leader of the Woman-suffrage movement, abolitionist, labor activist, **108**

Armstrong, Lance (1971-). American cyclist, triumphant cancer survivor went on to win the Tour de France for a record of seven consecutive times from 1999-2005, **58**

Arnold, H. (1886-1950). The only person to ever serve as both a General of the United States Army and a General of the United States Air Force, **68**

Ash, Mary Kay (1915-2001). Business executive, founder of Mary Kay Cosmetics, **45**

Bach, Richard (1936-). American writer, author of *Jonathan Livingston Seagull* (1977), *The Bridge Across Forever* (1984) and *One* (1989), **130**

Bacon, Francis (1561-1626). English philosopher, essayist, scientist and defender of the scientific revolution, **71**

Baez, Joan (1941-). American musician and singer, **217**

Bailey, Pearl (1918-1990). American actress, **215**

Baiul, Oksana (1977-). Ukrainian Figure skater, winner of the 1994 Olympic Gold Medal, **60**

Baldacci, David- 21st century suspense thriller novelist, author of *Split Second* (2004), **86**

Ball, Lucille (1911-1989). American actress, **121**

Banks, Ernie (1931-). American major league baseball player, Hall of Fame, **200**

Barnum, P. T. (1810-1891). Founder of the Barnum Circus which is known today as the Ringling Brothers & Barnum & Bailey Circus. He was known as "The Greatest Showman on Earth", **77, 97**

Barrymore, Drew (1975-). American actress, **96**

Battista, Orlando - Author of *Quotoons, A Speakers Dictionary* (1981), **57**

Baxter, Anne (1923-1985). American actress, **219**

Beamer, Lisa –wife of Todd Beamer, **128**

Beamer, Todd (1968-2001). Husband, father, American Hero, terrorist resister on United Airlines Flight 93, casualty of September 11th terrorist attacks on America, **231**

Beecher, Henry Ward (1813-1887). Clergyman, brother of Harriet Beecher Stowe, **71**

Beethoven, Ludwig von (1770-1827). German composer of classical music, **203**

Bell, Alexander Graham (1847-1922). Inventor of the telephone as well as numerous other inventions including the telegraph, phonograph and photophone, founder of the Bell Telephone Company, **78**

Berenson, Bernard, Author of *The Passionate Sightseer*, **140**

Berlin, Irving (1888-1989). Musician, composer of *White Christmas* and *God Bless America*, **76**

Berra, Yogi (1925-). American athlete, baseball player and baseball team manger, **48**

Bird, Larry (1956-). NBA basketball player, **152**

Bloch, Lionel, fictional film character, *Maid in Manhattan*, **190**

Bogart, Humphrey (1899-1957). American actor, **55**

Bolles, Richard Nelson - Author of *What Color is Your Parachute?* (1997), **89**

Bombeck, Erma (1927-1996). American journalist, **55**

Bonaparte, Napoleon (1769-1821). Dictator of France, Emperor of France, Conqueror, **75, 95**

Bono, Cher (1946-). American musician and performer, **94**

Boone, Daniel (1734-1820). American frontiersman & pioneer, **94**

Boswell, Nelson - Author of *Successful Living* (1976) and *Inner Peace, Inner Power* (1990), **69**

Brooks, Garth (1962-). American country singer, songwriter, **184**

Brooks, Mel (1926-). Actor, writer, director, comedian, **161**

Brothers, Dr. Joyce (1928-). Author of *How to Get Whatever You Want* (1980), *What Every Woman Should Know About Men* (1982), and *Positive Plus, The Practical Plan for Liking Yourself Better* (1994), **164**

Brown, Les – Author of *Live Your Dreams* (1994) and *It's Not Over Until You Win* (1988). International motivational speaker, labeled as a child as a “slow learner”, **40**

Bryan, William Jennings (1860-1925) Orator, politician, **110**

Buck, Pearl (1892-1973) Missionary, Author of over 70 books including *The Good Earth,* 1938 Nobel Prize for Literature, **168**

Buddha, (563- 483 B.C.E.) Philosopher, called "the Enlightened One" Spiritual founder of Buddhism, **38, 157**

Buffet, Warren (1930-). Businessman and investor, **154**

Burnett, Carol (1933-). American actress, comedian, **165**

Burns, George (1896- 1996). Comedian and actor, **159**

Byrd, Richard E. (1888-1957) Rear Admiral, American explorer, Antarctic explorer, **178**

Byrne, Robert, American author of *The Other 637 Best Things Anybody Ever Said* (1984), **92**

Cage, Nicolas (1964-). American actor, **179**

Caine, Michael (1933-) British actor, **189**

Canfield, Jack- Author of *The Success Principles: How to Get From Where You Are to Where You Want to Be* (2004) and *The Power of Focus* (2000), **211**

Cantor, Eddie (1892-1964) Comedian, **188**

Capote, Truman (1924-1984) Novelist, author of *In Cold Blood* and *Breakfast at Tiffany's*, **92**

Capra, Frank (1897-1991) American classic Film Director most known for *It's a Wonderful Life*, **180**

Carey, Mariah (1970-). Popular American singer, musician, listed in the Guinness Book of World Records for ability to hit the highest note and for possessing the largest vocal range A2 - G7#, **121, 230**

Carnegie, Andrew (1835-1919). American industrialist, king of the steel industry, **77**

Carnegie, Dale (1888-1955). U.S. author and teacher of self-improvement techniques, author of *How to Win Friends and Influence People*, (1936), **88**

Carrey, Jim (1962-). Actor, comedian, **59**

Carrol, Lewis (1832-1898). English author of *Alice's Adventures in Wonderland*, **78**

Carson, Johnny (1925-2005). Actor, comedian, talk show host television icon **153**

Carter-Scott, Cherie-PhD. Author of *If Life is a Game, These are the Rules* (1998), **224**

Cayce, Edgar (1877-1945). American psychic, **160**

Cervantes, aka Miguel de Cervantes Saavedra (1547-1616) Spanish novelist, author of *Don Quixote*, **73**

Chanel, Coco (1883-1971). French designer, **170**

Chaplin, Charlie (1889-1977). English born American actor and director. Famed in early cinema silent film era, **37**

Chesterfield, Lord (1694-1773). British statesman, **41**

Christ, Jesus see **Jesus, 90, 223**

Churchill, Sir Winston (1874-1965). British statesman, soldier, author, Prime Minister of the United Kingdom, **68, 213, 229**

Cicero, (106-43 B.C.). Roman orator, lawyer, politician and philosopher, **132**

Clinton, Bill (1946-) 42nd President of the United States of America, **101**

Collins, Marva – Founder of Westside Preparatory School, Author of *Values: Lighting the Candle of Excellence: A Practical Guide for the Family* (1996), **70**

Confucius (551-479 BC). Influential and respected Chinese philosopher, **37**

Cosby, Bill (1937-). American actor, comedian, **218**

Covey, Stephen - Author of The 7 *Habits of Highly Effective People* (1990), **227**

Crockett, Davy (1786-1836). American folk hero, explorer, **219**

Cummings, E. E. (1894-1962). American poet, **205**

Curie, Madam Marie (1867-1934) Chemist,Nobel laureate, **45**

Da Vinci, Leonardo (1452-1519). Italian Renaissance architect, inventor, engineer, sculptor, painter, genius, **198**

Dawson, Roger, Author of *The Secrets of Power Negotiating* (2005), **127**

Dean, James (1931-1955). American actor, performer *Rebel Without a Cause*, American legend, died tragically in a car accident, **214**

Dempsey, Jack (1895-1983). Famous boxer, **205**

De Vos, Richard - American businessman, Author of *Believe* (1991), Co-founder of Amway, Owner of The Orlando Magic, heart transplant recipient, father of 19 children (14 foreign adopted), **80**

Diana, Princess of Wales, (1961-1997). British Royalty, first wife of Charles, Prince of Wales, **53**

Dickinson, Emily (1830-1886). American Poet, **177**

Dion, Celine (1968-). American singer, musician, performer, **213**

Disney, Walt (1901-1966). Film animator, producer, founder of the entertainment empire known by his own name, The Walt Disney Company, **87, 185, 218**

Disraeli, Benjamin (1804-1881). England's first and only Jewish Prime Minister, **104**

Ditka, Coach Mike (1939-). Chicago Bears Coach, Member of NFL Hall of Fame, , Super Bowl XX Coach **134, 216**

Donovan, Robert J. - Author of *PT 109: John F. Kennedy in World War II Conflict and Crisis: The Presidency of Harry S. Truman* and, **106**

Dufresne, Andy, fictional character, *Shawshank Redemption*, **100**

Durante, Jimmy (1893-1980). Comedian, **118**

Dyer, Dr. Wayne W.-Author of *Manifest Your Destiny* (1997), *The Nine Spiritual Principles for Getting Everything You Want* (1999), **109**

Dylan, Bob (1941-). American musician, popular songwriter, **50**

Earhart, Amelia (1848-1937). American aviator, First person to fly solo across the Pacific Ocean, **203**

Edison, Thomas Alva (1847-1931). Called the greatest inventor in history, had only three months of formal schooling, changed the lives of millions of people, patented 1093 inventions in his lifetime including the electric light, phonograph and motion picture device, **86**

Einstein, Albert (1879-1955). Recognized as one of the greatest physicists of all time, **72**

Eliot, George, the official pen name of British author, Mary Ann Evans (1819-1880), **75**

Ellington, Duke (1899-1974). American Jazz composer, **201**

Elvis, also known as Elvis Presley (1935-1977). Popular American singer, **61**

Emerson, Ralph Waldo (1803-1882). Philosopher, poet, a major figure in American literature, called the "Sage of Concord", **66**

Feather, William (1889-1981). Author of *As We Were Saying* (1921), **73**

Fields, W.C. (1888-1946) Comedian, stage, radio and early film actor, **103, 169**

Firestone, Harvey S. (1868-1930). American businessman, tire manufacturer, **154**

Fitzgerald, Ella (1918-1996). American Jazz singer, winner of 13 Grammy awards, **223**

Fitzgerald, F. Scott (1896-1940). Novelist, Author of *The Great Gatsby*, **155**

Forbes, B.C. –Author of *Keys to Success or Personal Efficiency* (2003) and *How to Get the Most Out of Business* (2003), **71**

Forbes, Malcom S. (1919-1990). Publisher, sportsman, **82**

Ford, Betty (1918-). Former First Lady of the United States, wife of the 38th President of the United States of America, humanitarian, breast cancer survivor, recovered from addiction to alcohol and prescription drugs, **43**

Ford, Gerald (1913-2006). The 38th President of the United States of America, **134**

Ford, Harrison (1942-). American actor, **169**

Ford, Henry (1863-1947). Inventor, American industrialist, pioneer automobile manufacturer, **64, 69**

Frank, Anne (1929-1945). Jewish schoolgirl, diarist, *The Diary of Anne Frank* was published after her death in a Nazi concentration camp, **171**

Frankl, Viktor (1905-1997). M.D., .PhD., concentration camp survivor, Author of 32 books including *Man's Search for Meaning* (1985), **79, 146**

Franklin, Aretha (1942-). American singer of Gospel, Soul and Rhythm & Blues, **119**

Franklin, Benjamin (1706-1790). Statesman, revolutionary leader, printer, writer, scientist. Often called the "Wisest" American, **59, 148, 173**

Frederick, Carl –Author of *You Don't have to Rehearse to Be Yourself (*1978), and *est, Playing the Game * The New Way (*The Game of Life)*. (2003), **69**

Frost, Robert (1874-1963). American poet, recipient of four Pulitzer Prizes, **129**

Fuller, R. Buckminster (1895-1983). Inventor, designer, architect, writer, visionary, patent holder for the first patent for Geodesic domes, **38**

Fuller, Thomas (1608-1661). English clergyman and historian, **81**

Galbraith, John Kenneth, (1908-). Canadian born North American economist and author of *Money, Whence It Came, Where It Went* and *A Short History of Financial Euphoria*, **113**

Gandhi, Mohandas, aka Mohatma Gandhi (1869-1948). Hindu leader, non-violent revolutionary, **46**

Garfield, James A. (1831-1881). 20th President of the United States of America, the first left-handed President, **49**

Garland, Judy (1922-1969). American actress since age 12, died of an accidental overdose, **176**

Gates, Bill (1955-). American businessman, co-founder and chairman of Microsoft Corp, philanthropist, **175**

Gawain, Shakti – Author of *Creative Visualization* (1998), **40**

Getty, J. Paul (1892-1976). American industrialist, founder of Getty Oil Company, **141**

Gibran, Kahlil (1883-1931). Lebanese poet, philosopher, artist, author of *The Prophet* (1923), **107**

Gifford, Frank (1930-). Athlete, pro-football player, sports announcer, **108**

Giovanni, Nikki (1943-). Civil Rights and Black Arts Movement poet, **117**

Givens, Charles, U.S. Businessman, Author of *Wealth Without Risk* (1988), **152**

Gleason, Jackie (1916-1987). American actor, comedian, **182**

Goethe, Johann Wolfgang von (1749-1832). German playwright, author of *Faust*, **131**

Goldberg, Whoopi (1949-). American actress, **174**

Goldsmith, Oliver (1730-1774). Irish physician, author of *She Stoops to Conquer*, **171**

Goldwyn, Samuel, One of the founders of Metro-Goldwyn, Mayer Production Co. (MGM), **194**

Graham, Stedman – American entrepreneur, educator and author of *Teens Can Make It Happen* (2000), **195**

Gray, Dr. John- Author of *Men Are From Mars, Women Are from Venus* (2004), *How to Get What You Want and Want What You Have* (2001), **132**

Greene, Bob - Journalist, author of *Get With the Program: Getting Real About Your Weight, Health and Emotional Well Being* (2004), **49**

Greenberg, Sidney - Respected Jewish rabbi, author of *Lessons forLiving* (1985), **74**

Gretzky, Wayne (1961-). Canadian Professional ice hockey player, executive director of 2002 Olympic Gold winning hockey team, **176**

Groban, Josh (1982-). American singer, **193**

Guccione, J. E. (1954-). Author of *The Greater Adventures of Humpty Dumpty (*1995*), The Power of Choice* (2007), **117**

Halas, George (1895-1985). American football player, coach, Co-founder of the NFL, (National Football League), **220**

Hamilton, Alexander (1757-1804). The first Secretary of the Treasury of the United States of America, **51**

Hamilton, Scott (1958-). American athlete, World Figure Skating Champion (1984), **105**

Hammer, Armand (1898-1990). American Industrialist, the first CEO of Occidental Petroleum Company, **177**

Hammerstein, Oscar II (1895-1960). Writer/producer of Broadway musicals: *The Sound of Music, Carousel, Oklahoma, South Pacific,The King & I*, **179**

Hanks, Tom (1956-). American actor, producer, director, **119**

Hansen, Grace - Politician, humorist, **53**

Harlow, Jean (1911-1937). American actress, **101**

Harris, Thomas A. –Author of *I'm OK-You're OK* (1967), **162**

Harvey, Paul (1918-). Well-known radio personality, news Commentator, best known for his broadcast entitled "*The Rest of the Story*", **208**

Hastie, Judge William (1904-1976). Attorney, judge, magistrate, first African-American appointed as a Federal Circuit judge, **56**

Hawthrone, Nathaniel (1804-1864). American Novelist, *The Scarlet Letter* and *The House of the Seven Gables*, **120**

Hayes, Helen (1900-1993). American actress, **100**

Hemingway, Ernest (1899-1961). Novelist, *The Old Man & The Sea,* winner of the Nobel Prize and the Pulitzer Prize, suicide victim, **168**

Henry, O. (1862-1910). American writer, convicted and sentenced for embezzlement, released from prison after five years and then began a writing career. Author of *The Gift of the Magi* and other works, **107**

Herzl, Theodore (1860-1904). Viennese journalist and founder of modern political Zionism, **167**

Hill, Napoleon (1883-1970). Author of *Think and Grow Rich* (1960), **80, 83, 143, 191**

Hilton, Conrad (1887-1979). An American businessman "the biggest hotel man in the world", **41, 72**

Holmes, Oliver Wendell (1809-1894). U.S. poet, novelist, essayist, jurist and physician, **67, 96**

Hook, Dr. - Popular U. S. cult band, **180**

Hoover, Herbert (1874-1964). 31st President of the United States of America, **98**

Horace (65 BC-8 BC). Roman poet, **220**

Hubbard, Elbert (1865-1915) American philosopher and writer, former soap salesman, printer and publisher, **88, 111**

Huxley, Aldous (1894-1963). Author of *Brave New World* (1946), *The Doors of Perception (1954) and Heaven and Hell*, (1956), **138**

Iacocca, Lee (1924-). American Industrialist, savior of the Chrysler Corporation, **99**

Irving, Washington (1783-1859). American author of *The Legend of Sleepy Hollow* and *Rip Van Winkle,* **81**

Jackson, Bo (1962-). American athlete, baseball out-fielder and football running back, Heisman Trophy winner (1985), **124**

Jackson, Jesse (1941-). Minister, Civil Rights activist, **147**

James, William (1842-1910). Acclaimed as a foremost philosopher, psychologist, author of *The Will to Believe & Other Essays in Popular Philosophy* (1897), **112, 133**

Jefferson, Thomas (1743-1826). 3rd President of the United States of America, **70, 104**

Jesus of Nazareth aka Jesus Christ (4 BC-29 AD). The Basis for and Source of the Christian religion, The Son of God, **90, 223**

Joel, Billy (1949-). American singer, songwriter, pianist, **225**

Johnson, Spencer, M.D. – Author of *The One Minute Manager* (1983) and *Who Moved My Cheese?* (1998), **137**

Jones, Shirley (1933-). American actress, **183**

Joplin, Janis (1943-1970) American Singer, songwriter, **165**

Jordan, Michael (1960-). American athlete, leading scorer in the NBA, called "the Best Basketball Player in history", **125**

Joyce, James (1882-1941). Irish Novelist, Author of *Ulysses*, **50**

Judd, H. Stanley- Author of *Think Rich* (1978), **84**

Kazan, Elia (1909-2003). Turkish born director, American stage and film, **103**

Keller, Helen (1880-1968). Author, educator, blind and deaf from an illness at 19 months old, overcame her disabilities to become an outstanding example of a person who overcame and conquered physical handicaps, **42**

Kennedy, Bobby, a.k.a. Robert Kennedy (1925-1968). Legislator, **62**

Kennedy, John F. a.k.a. "JFK" (1917-1963). 35th President of the United States, **145, 166**

Kennedy, Rose Fitzgerald (1890-1995). Matriarch of the Kennedy family, the longest-lived presidential parent in history, mother of "JFK", the 35th President of the USA, **140**

King, Martin Luther (1929-1968). Clergyman, Civil Rights Leader, **139, 167**

King Stanislaus I of Poland (1677-1766). King of Poland, who abdicated his throne in 1736, **94**

Kipling, Rudyard (1865-1936). British author and poet, author of *The Jungle Book* (1894) and *Captains Courageous* (1897), recipient of the 1907 Nobel Prize for Literature, **222**

Kissinger, Henry A.(1923-). American statesman, diplomat. **51**

Knight, Philip H. – Chairman & CEO of Nike Inc., **134**

Korda, Michael (1919-1973). Author of *Man to Man* (1996), a book about prostate cancer, **52, 66**

Krishnamurti, Jiddu (1895-1986). Indian philosopher and Spiritual leader, **149**

L'Amour, Louis (1908-1988). American author of western frontier novels, **124**

Lakein, Alan - Author of *How to Get Control of Your Time and Your Life* (1996), **190**

Lama, Dalai (1935-). The highest religious leader of Tibetan Buddhism, **120**

Landers, Ann (1918-2002). Newspaper columnist, **46, 169**

Landry, Tom (1924-2000). NFL football player and coach, **172**

Lao-tzu (circa 6th century BC). First philosopher of Chinese Taoism and allegedly the author of *Tao-te-Ching,* **89**

Lasorda, Tommy (1927-). Baseball manager, Member of Baseball Hall of Fame, **63**

Latifah, Queen (1970-). Rap musician, actress, **61**

Lawrence, D. H. (1885-1930). British author of the controversial *Lady's Chatterley's Lover,* **181**

Lee, Bruce (1940-1973). Martial arts expert, actor, **47**

Leider, Richard J.- Author of *The Power of Purpose* (1997), **142**

Lemmon, Jack (1925-2001) Actor, director, cancer victim, **47**

Lennon, John (1940-1980). English songwriter, musician, guitarist for *The Beatles*, died tragically, **72**

Lewis, C. S. (1898-1963). Irish author of *The Lion, The Witch and The Wardrobe*, **54**

Lewis, Jerry (1926-). American comedian, actor, notable fund raiser, host of the annual charitable telethon for the Muscular Dystrophy Association, **48**

Lincoln, Abraham ((1809-1865). 16th President of the United States of America, **45, 114**

Lindbergh, Charles (1902-1974). American aviator famous for the first non-stop flight across the Atlantic Ocean, **92**

Lloyd, Chris Evert (1954-). American athlete, professional tennis player, **93**

Lloyd-George, David (1863-1945) 1st Earl, British Prime Minister, Liberal Statesman, **196**

Lombardi, Vincent T. (1913-1970). NFL coach, most known for the all time record of the most wins. The famed Super Bowl trophy is named in his honor, **66**

Lopez, Jennifer a.k.a. "J Lo" (1970-). Puerto Rican-American actress, singer, dancer and fashion designer, **194**

Luce, Clare Booth Luce (1903-1987). American ambassador and playwright, associate editor of *Vogue* and the *Vanity Fair* Magazines, **166**

MacArthur, Douglas (1880-1964). General of the U.S. Army, Medal of Honor recipient, **55**

Machiavelli, Niccolo (1468-1527) Italian diplomat, political philosopher and political scientist, author of *The Prince,* (An instruction book for rulers), **46**

MacLaine, Shirley (1934-). American actress, Author of *Going Within* (1990) and *Out on a Limb (*1996), **196**

Madonna, a.k.a. Madonna Ciccone (1958-). Singer, songwriter, the queen of pop music, actress, said to have an IQ of 140, **184**

Malcolm X (1925-1965). American activist, militant black nationalist leader, **52**

Mandela, Nelson (1918-). First black President of South Africa, imprisoned for opposing apartheid, **145, 226**

Mandino, Og - Author of *The Greatest Salesman in the World* (1983), **86**

Mann, Horace (1796-1859) American educationist and abolitionist, **95**

Mantle, Mickey (1931-1995). American baseball player, Member of the U. S. Baseball Hall of Fame, **52**

Mao Tse-tung aka Mao Zedong (1893-1976). Leader of the Communist Party of China from 1935, instrumental in the founding of the People's Republic of China, **56**

Marden, Orison Swett - Author of *The Miracle of a Right Thought and the Divinity of Desire* (1996) and *He Who Thinks He Can* (2003), **82**

Marovitz, Judge Abraham Lincoln (1905-2001). Senior Federal Judge for the Northern District of Illinois, USA, **135**

Maxwell, John –Author of *The 21 Irrefutable Laws of Leadership* (1998) and *Developing the Leader Within You* (2000), **157**

McCartney, Paul (1942-). Member of *The Beatles*, pianist, bassist, guitarist, singer, songwriter, **123**

McCullough, Mamie–Author of *I Can, You Can Too!* (1981), **130**

McFerrin, Bobby (1950-). Popular jazz singer, *Don't Worry, Be Happy* (1988), **101**

McKay, Matthew – Author of *Self Esteem: A Proven Program of Cognitive Techniques for Accessing, Improving and Maintaining your Self Esteem* (2000). **131**

McWilliams, Peter -Author of *How To Survive the Loss of a Love* (1976), **57**

Meir, Golda (1898-1978). Russian born Israeli politician, **183**

Meyer, Coach Ray (1913-2006). Dc Paul University's legendary Basketball coach, **135**

Michelangelo a.k.a. Michelangelo Buonarroti (1475-1564). Renaissance painter, sculptor, poet and architect, **202**

Minnelli, Liza (1946-). American singer, actress, **117**

Moody, Dwight L. a.k.a. DL Moody (1837-1899). American evangelist, publisher, founder of the Moody Church, Moody Bible Institute and the Moody Press, **67**

Mother Teresa, (1910-1997). Leader of the Order of the Missionaries of Charity, 1979 Nobel Peace Prize Laureate, **133**

Murphy, John- Author of *Infinite Power for Richer Living* (1969), **129**

Napoleon see Bonaparte, Napoleon, **75, 95**

Navratilova, Martina (1956-). Czechoslovakian-American Tennis Champion, **148**

Newton, Sir Isaac (1642-1727). English alchemist, mathematician, scientist and philosopher, **186**

Nicklaus, Jack (1940-). American PGA Champion golfer, **93**

Nightingale, Florence (1820-1910) The pioneer of modern nursing, **211**

Nixon, Richard M. (1913-1994). 37th President of the United States of America. Resigned facing certain impeachment so that the "process of healing which is so desperately needed in America might begin", **74, 105**

Norvell- Author *of The Magic of Prosperity Magic* (1981), purported to be an advisor to some of the world's most famous people, **138**

O'Donnell, Rosie (1962-). Actress, talk show host, **228**

O'Hara, Scarlett- High-tempered, strong-willed Southern belle, fictional character from *GoneWith the Wind* (1939), **109**

Olivier, Sir Laurence (1907-1989). English actor and director, **118**

Onassis, Aristotle (1906-1975). Greek shipping magnate, **151**

Oprah, a.k.a. Oprah Winfrey (1954-). TV host, actress, producer, philanthropist, one of the most successful women in history, sexual abuse survivor, **39, 102, 204**

Ornish, Dr. Dean –First cardiac researcher, clinician to offer documented proof that heart disease can be halted or reversed by lifestyle changes. Author of *Dr. Dean Ornish's Program for reversing Heart Disease* (1995), **144, 150**

Ortega y Gasset, Jose, (1883-1995). Spanish philosopher, author of *Revolt of the Masses*, **50**

Osborn, Alex - Author of *Your Creative Power* (1948), **136**

Palmer, Arnold (1929-). American PGA Champion Golfer, **115**

Parks, Rosa (1913-2005). Became a national symbol Civil Rights activist in 1955 when tired after a long day of work, she refused to give up her seat to a white man, **111**

Parton, Dolly (1946-). Popular American country singer, songwriter, actress, **178**

Pasteur, Louis (1822-1895). French scientist, **116**

Paterno, Joe (1926-). Head football Coach Penn State University, **44**

Patton, General George S. (1885-1945). One of the most colorful American Generals of WWII, nickname "Old Blood and Guts" **75, 85**

Peale, Norman Vincent (1898-1993) clergyman author of *The Power of Positive Thinking* (1952), **36**

Pelzer, Dave- Author of Help Yourself (2000). Survivor of extreme child abuse, **224**

Pendergrass, Teddy (1950-). American musician, **91**

Perot, H. Ross (1930-). Business executive, political figure, **62**

Piatka, Nadja - Canadian rags to riches entrepreneur, President and Founder of Nadja Foods, author of *Joy of Losing Weight* (1992), **221**

Picasso, Pablo (1881-1973). Artist, Master of 20th century art, Founder of Cubism, **207**

Pickford, Mary (1893-1979). American actress, **191**

Ponder, Catherine Author of *Open Your Mind to Prosperity* (1971), **196**

Pope John Paul II (1920- 2005). Polish born religious leader of the Catholic Church, First Slavic born Pope in history, author, peacemaker, shepherd, missionary to the world, **209**

Powell, Retired General Colin (1937-). The 65th United States Secretary of State, **187**

Queen Elizabeth I of England. (1533-1603). Queen of England, the last Tudor ruler, **99**

Queen Victoria of the United Kingdom, (1819-1901). Queen of England, one of the greatest rulers in English history, ruled for a record sixty-three years, seven months, and two days (6/20/1837 to 1/22/1901). She was also Empress of India, **84**

Raleigh, Sir Walter (1552-1618). English poet, writer, explorer, Spymaster to Elizabeth I, **122**

Rather, Dan (1931-). American news anchorman, **98**

Redenbacher, Orville, (1907-1995). Natural popcorn entrepreneur, **137**

Reeve, Dana (1961-2006) American actress, activist for disability causes, wife of the late Christopher Reeve, **230**

Reeve, Christopher (1952-2004) American actor (*Superman*), activist, author of *Still Me* (1999), **54, 59, 114, 155**

Robbins, Anthony –Motivational mogul, Author of *Unlimited Power* (1986), **143**

Roberts, Wess –Author of *Straight A's Never Made Anybody Rich* (1992), **126**

Rockefeller, John D. (1839-1937). American capitalist and philanthropist, **131**

Rockwell, Norman (1894-1978). Painter, illustrator, **60**

Rogers, Kenny (1938-). American Country singer, actor, **98, 193**

Rogers, Will (1879-1935). Actor, humorist, straight-talking cowboy philosopher, **113**

Rooney, Andy (1919-). American journalist and commentator, **157**

Roosevelt, Eleanor (1884-1962). Former First Lady of the United States, wife of the 32nd President of the United States of America, reformer, humanitarian, writer, said to be the most active First Lady in all of American history, **44, 85, 116**

Roosevelt, Franklin Delano also known as “FDR” (1882-1945). The 32nd President of the United States of America. polio victim, physically challenged President of the United States of America, **73, 115, 139**

Roosevelt, Theodore (1858-1919). 26th President of the United States of America, **104**

Saint-Exupery, Antoine de (1900-1944). Adventurer, illustrator and author of *The Little Prince*, **49**

Salk, Jonas (1914-1955). American Scientist, inventor of the polio vaccine, **53**

Sandburgh, Carl (1878-1967). American poet, **177**

Saradon, Susan (1946-). American actress, **195**

Sassoon, Vidal – American cosmetologist, **188**

Sawyer, Diane (1945-). American journalist, **222**

Sayers, Gayle - American athlete, football player, famous left-handed person, **149**

Schucman, Helen -“scribe” of *A Course in Miracles* (1975), **70**

Schultz, Charles M. (1922-2000). American cartoonist, creator of the *Peanuts* comic strip, **170**

Schumann, Robert (1810-1956). German Musical composer and pianist, **122**

Schwab, Charles (1937-). American businessman, **172**

Schwarzenegger, Arnold (1947-). Bodybuilder, actor, Governor of the State of California, **64**

Schwartz, David J.-Author of *The Magic of Thinking Big*, (1987), 77

Seneca, Lucius Annaeus (3BC-65AD). Roman philosopher, dramatist, **65, 79, 93**

Seuss, Dr., pseudonym of Theodor Seuss Geisel (1904-1991). American author of *The Cat in the Hat,* (1957) and 239 other books, illustrator, poet and filmmaker, recipient of a special Pulitzer Prize for Lifetime Achievement (1984), **181**

Seymour, Jane (1951-) Actress, author of *Remarkable Changes: Turning Life's Challenges Into Opportunities* (2003), **36**

Shakespeare, William (1564-1616). Dramatist (*Romeo & Juliet, Hamlet, Macbeth,* etc.), **79, 109, 132**

Shakur, Tupac (1971-1996). American Gangsta Rap artist, fatally shot in Las Vegas, NV, **76**

Shaw, George Bernard (1856-1950). Dramatist, **60, 110, 185**

Sheen, Bishop Fulton (1895-1979). Renowned Catholic bishop and host of an inspiring television series called *Life is Worth Living*, author of over 60 books, **57**

Shriver, Maria (1955-). Veteran TV News Report, gubernatorial wife, mother, author of *Ten Things I Wish I'd Known Before I Went Into The Real World* (2000), **139**

Sills, Beverly (1929-) American Opera star, **156**

Socrates, (469-399 B.C.E.) Greek moralist and philosopher, **135**

Sosa, Sammy (1968-). Major League baseball player, **204**

Springsteen, Bruce (1949-) American singer and songwriter, **153**

St. Augustine (354-430 AD). Professor, Catholic Bishop of Hippo, writer, attested to be the very first autobiographer, **214**

St. Frances DeSales (16567-1662). Catholic priest, orator, writer, director of souls, Bishop, founder of the Order of the Visitation, **65**

St. John, Noah – Author of *Permission to Succeed* (1999), Founder and CEO of The Success Clinic of America, **83**

St. Peter of Alcantara (1499-1562) Catholic priest from Spain, **217**

Stallone, Sylvester (1946-). American actor, **197**

Stanley, Thomas MD-Author of *The Millionaire Mind* (2000), **129**

Steiger, Rod (1925-2002). American actor, **198**

Stepanek, Mattie J. T. (1990-2004). Poet, peacemaker, philosopher, muscular dystrophy victim, author of *Heartsongs (2002), Hope Through Heartsongs (2002)* and other books of poems, **192**

Stern, Daniel (1957-). American actor and director, **204**

Stevenson, Robert Louis (1850-1894). Scottish novelist, Author of *Treasure Island* and *Kidnapped,* **87, 215**

Sting (1951-) English musician, former lead singer of 1970's Rock Trio *The Police*, **185**

Stone, Sharon (1958-) American actress, **200**

Stone, W. Clement (1902- 2002). American businessman, author of *Success Through a Positive Mental Attitude* (1960), **199**

Strand, Mark (1934-). Poet Laureate, Pulitzer Prize for Poetry for *Blizzard of One* (1999), **199**

Swanson, Gloria (1899-1983). American actress, **102**

Swayze, Patrick (1952-). American actor, **136**

Taylor, Elizabeth (1932-) English American actress, Dame of the British Empire, devoted advocate for AIDS–related charities, **164**

Thatcher, Margaret (1925-). British politician, first woman Prime Minister of the United Kingdom, Baroness, **151**

Thomas, R. Dave (1932-2002). American businessman, founder and co-chairman of *Wendy's Old Fashioned Hamburgers/Wendy Intl. Inc.,* adopted as an infant, a lifetime advocate for adoption, High School drop-out at age 15, GED recipient in 1993, **74**

Thoreau, Henry David (1817-1862). Naturalist, author of *Civil Disobedience* (1849) and *Walden* (1854), **106, 150**

Thurber, James (1894-1961). American humorist, cartoonist, **48**

Tracy, Brian- Motivational author of *Goals! How to Get Everything You Want-Faster Than You Ever Thought Possible* (2003), *Getting Rich Your Own Way* (2004) and *Maximum Achievement* (1995), **158**

Tracy, Spencer (1900-1967). American actor, **150**

Trudeau, Pierre Elliot (1919-2000). The 15th Prime Minister of Canada, **122**

Truman, Harry S. (1884-1972). 33rd President of the United States of America, **76, 162**

Trump, Donald (1946-). American businessman, **163**

Turner, Ted (1938-) American businessman, founder of CNN, **154**

Twain, Mark (1835-1910). Popular American humorist, author of *Tom Sawyer* and *Adventures of Huckleberry Finn*, **81, 163**

Twain, Shania (1965-). Canadian singer and songwriter, **159**

U. S. Army Corp. of Engineers-the world's premier public engineering organization, **128**

Van Gough, Vincent (1853-1890). Dutch Painter, artist, suicide victim, **202**

Virgil, (70BC-19BC). Famous poet of ancient Rome, **142**

Vitale, Dr. Joe- Author of *The Attractor Factor: 5 Easy Steps for Creating Wealth (or Anything Else) From the Inside Out* (2005), *Life's Missing Instruction Manual: The Guidebook You Should Have Been Given at Birth* (2006), **127**

Voltaire (1694-1778). French Enlightenment writer, **197**

Waitley, Denis- Motivational speaker and producer, author of *Seeds of Greatness* (1984) and *The Psychology of Winning* (1992), **221, 227**

Walsch, Neale Donald –Author of *Recreating Your Self* (2000), *The Complete Conversations With God* (2005). **231**

Walters, Barbara (1931-). American television commentator, talk show host, **91**

Walton, Sam (1919-1992). American businessman, founder of Wal-Mart, **144**

Warhol, Andy (1927-1987). Artist, **207**

Washington, George (1732-1976). The 1st President of the United States of America, **208**

Wayne, John (1907-1979). American actor most noted for Western movies, **210**

Webster, Daniel (1782-1852). Statesman., **63**

Wells, H. G. (1866-1946). English author of *The War of the Worlds* and *The Time Machine*, **210**

Welles, Orson (1915-1985). Actor, director, producer, **106**

Welk, Lawrence (1903-1992). Musician, band leader, TV producer of *The Lawrence Welk Show*, **137**

West, Mae (1883-1980). American actress, **212**

Whitney, Willis R. (1868-1958). First director of GE (General Electric) research laboratory, **65**

Wilde, Oscar (1854-1900). Irish poet, playwright and author of *Picture of Dorian Gray* (1891), **111**

Wilder, Laura Ingalls (1867-1957). Author of *Little House on the Prairie*, **96**

Williams, Robin (1951-). American actor, comedian, Oscar winner, reported to have a bipolar disorder, **187**

Williams, Tennessee (1911-1983). Playwright, Pulitzer Prize for drama 1948 & 1955, survivor of gay bashing., **97**

Williams, Vanessa (1963-). 1st Black Miss America, resigned early due to pornography scandal, eventually returned to fame as a popular singer, **201**

Williamson, Marianne - Author of *A Return to Love* (1992), **126**

Winfrey- see Oprah, **39, 102, 204**

Wooden, Coach John (1910-). "Coach of the Century" with an unbreakable winning record. Recipient of the Presidential Medal of Freedom (2003), author, lecturer, **63, 229**

Wonder, Stevie (1950-) American soul singer, musician, **216**

Wright, Frank Lloyd (1869-1959). Renowned architect, **107**

Xerxes also known as Ahasuerus- King of Persia reigning from 485-465 BC, **118**

Xi Zhi, (1130-1200). Chinese neo-Confucian philosopher, **112**

Yoda (fictional character), The Jedi Master, *Star Wars*, **37**

Zappa, Frank (1940-). American Rock musician, **108**

Zeppelin, Led –British blues rock band, **186**

Ziglar, Zig - Author of *Over the Top* (1997), **80**

Zuflet, Jack M.- Author of *The DNA of Success* (2000), **225**

Epilogue

Why Now?

"We are called to heal the broken,
to be hope for the poor."

As we mark our way along this new millennium, we would be wise to consider the following. Two-thirds of the seniors who have ever lived in the history of the world are alive today. Many of the current senior citizens have lived through two World Wars, The Great Depression, The Cold War, and several oil crises. They fear yet another World War.

In the 1999-2000 academic year, more than 1,235,000 bachelor's degrees were conferred by American colleges and universities. A sample of estimates of the career placement offices of various state universities put the rate unemployment of recent graduates at 12-16%. It is expected to get worse.

A recent 40 year low in interest rates has enticed many American's to refinance their mortgages, saving American households millions of dollars on their mortgage payments. The overall levels of consumer debt have also risen to record levels. Concurrently, the United States has seen a staggering increase in personal bankruptcy filings. Over 1.3 million people per year have filed for bankruptcy in each of the past five years. It is estimated that one in every twenty two families will reorganize in some form of bankruptcy.

More than 570,000 companies were created in the United States in 2001. The failure rate for small business is dismal. Current statistics indicate that less than 25% of start-up companies survive beyond 36 months yet the majority of companies listed on the NASDAQ stock exchange are less then 15 years old.

In their quest for better health, American's spend an average of $873 per person per year on healthcare and medical expenses. Each year approximately 1,380,000 new cases of cancer are diagnosed, excluding about 900,000 cases of non-melanoma skin cancer, the most common and curable form of human cancer. In the U.S., cancer mortality is estimated to account for 560,000 deaths this year. Every two minutes somewhere in the world, a woman is diagnosed with breast cancer. Those figures though are only the second leading cause of death. Heart disease deaths claim the greatest percentage.

Depression is nearly at epidemic levels. It is estimated that in the U.S., suicide accounts for at least 25,000 deaths each year. It is highly possible that closer to 75,000 American kill themselves each year as many suicides are reported as accidents or illnesses.

In 1999, there was one divorce for every two marriages in the United States, giving the U.S. a "crude" divorce rate of 50%. People between the ages of 25 and 39 make up 60% of all divorces. It is further estimated that more than four million couples "cohabitation" without the formality of marriage. For this reason, divorce statistics are no longer collected in America.

In 2000 there were approximately 281 million people living in the United States. It was estimated that the world population exceeded 6 billion! The U.S. population represents less than 5% of the world's population. Statistics for all of the above for the population of the world are unknown.

In just the past one hundred years, the world has seen the creation of more inventions and innovations than in any other period of time in history. Many previously dreaded diseases and ailments have been cured. It is our opinion that the BEST IS YET TO COME! It is our intention to provide the tools to support those who will lead us into those bright new horizons! We sincerely hope that mankind will never lose sight of the one precious commodity at the heart of its very being - the gift of free will and thereby *the power of choice*! We hope that this volume will serve as a gentle reminder of such.

The only person
who can pull you
out of this is

YOU !

H. D.

This is **NOT** THE END

It is The Beginning!

H. D. & FRIENDS
Stories of Triumph

Just as "H.D." discovered that he indeed had choices, many of our friends have stories of how they navigated through the rough waters of life to reach their own personal triumphs. Perhaps you know of someone who had to overcome great obstacles on their road to personal greatness or someone who may have "had it all" (as they "sat on their walls") until some unforeseen circumstance caused them to fall from their high and mighty position. Others may have been sitting in the mud for all their lives, feeling like a dud, until they chose to pick themselves up and had the courage to reach for a star. "H.D." is not the only one in the world who has had to pick up the best and leave all the rest. Many of our friends have told us that they too have stories of HOPE to encourage others.

We invite you to share your stories with us.

Tell us how you (or someone you know) dealt with and overcame the loss of love or the loss of a job, a physical or financial challenge, a serious illness or a bad attitude, addiction or dependency, discrimination or self sabotage or anything else that may have caused them to fall from their wall, stumble on their path or get stuck in the mud.

Send a copy of your story to us at:

H.D. & Friends
c/o Joyce Guccione
4238B N. Arlington Heights Rd.
Suite 370
Arlington Hts. IL 60004
Fax: 847-394-0215
Email: HD@optimysticminds.com

We do intend to publish several collections of the stories submitted to H.D. & Friends and we will be sure to credit you for your submission.

Thanks for sharing your story of hope with the world!

You can also contact us at the address above for information regarding H.D.'s products (books, audio tapes, teaching aids, posters, promotional items, etc.) as well as for information about scheduling speaking engagements or training programs conducted by H.D.'s friends and affiliates.

See us at:
www.optimysticminds.com

Many thanks to MOTHER GOOSE
for giving me a reason to
look for a happy ending.

Many thanks to
"the Voice within"
for showing me
how to find it!

For Thine is the Kingdom,
and the Power, and The Glory.
Now and Forever.
Amen.